Bruce Lee

A Comprehensive Biography of Bruce Lee

(Isometric Exercise Routines for a Bruce Lee Body)

Gary Lucchesi

Published By **Kate Sanders**

Gary Lucchesi

All Rights Reserved

Introverts: How Introverts Can Find Love and Have Better Relationships (Practical Tools to Leverage Your Strengths and Expand Your Network)

ISBN 978-1-7782374-8-5

No part of this guidebook shall be reproduced in any form without permission in writing from the publisher except in the case of brief quotations embodied in critical articles or reviews.

Legal & Disclaimer

The information contained in this book is not designed to replace or take the place of any form of medicine or professional medical advice. The information in this book has been provided for educational & entertainment purposes only.

The information contained in this book has been compiled from sources deemed reliable, and it is accurate to the best of the Author's knowledge; however, the Author cannot guarantee its accuracy and validity and cannot be held liable for any errors or omissions. Changes are periodically made to this book. You must consult your doctor or get professional medical advice before using any of the suggested remedies, techniques, or information in this book.

Upon using the information contained in this book, you agree to hold harmless the Author from and against any damages, costs, and expenses, including any legal fees potentially resulting from the application of any of the information provided by this guide. This disclaimer applies to any damages or injury caused by the use and application, whether directly or indirectly, of any advice or information presented, whether for breach of contract, tort, negligence, personal injury, criminal intent, or under any other cause of action.

You agree to accept all risks of using the information presented inside this book. You need to consult a professional medical practitioner in order to ensure you are both able and healthy enough to participate in this program.

Table Of Contents

Chapter 1: Hong Kong Childhoods 1

Chapter 2: Journey to San Francisco 15

Chapter 3: Philosophy in the Decrease Back of the Art 29

Chapter 4: The Green Hornet Kato Rises 43

Chapter 5: Making Of a Martial Arts Classic 55

Chapter 6: Bruce Lee's Martial Arts Philosophy 69

Chapter 7: Meeting Linda Lee 84

Chapter 8: Roots in San Francisco 98

Chapter 9: Early Challenges and Influences 104

Chapter 10: Martial Arts Odyssey 109

Chapter 11: Enter the Dragon 126

Chapter 12: The Private Bruce Lee 137

Chapter 13: Legacy in Martial Arts 160

Chapter 14: Pop Culture References and Homage 173

Chapter 15: Bruce Lee's Unfinished Business 177

Chapter 16: Reflecting On The Legend . 181

Chapter 1: Hong Kong Childhoods

In the bustling streets of Nineteen Forties Hong Kong, amidst the clamor and colorful shades of a metropolis teeming with lifestyles, the story of Bruce Lee began. Born on November 27, 1940, as Lee Jun-fan, he entered the sector in the hour of the dragon, in a town that comes to be a melting pot of cultures, traditions, and ideologies. This complicated tapestry of early research in Hong Kong formed the legend Bruce Lee changed into to end up, mixing the impacts of East and West in a manner as dynamic because the individual himself.

Lee's mother and father, Lee Hoi-Chuen and Grace Ho, supplied culturally wealthy surroundings. His father, a famend Cantonese opera celebrity, and his mom, of Eurasian descent, brought young Bruce to the arena of performing arts early on. But the streets of Hong Kong provided him his first actual instructions in resilience and determination. The metropolis, vibrant yet fraught with worrying situations, changed into a place in which Bruce found to navigate complexities a protracted way past his years.

Imagine a more youthful Bruce, his eyes large with curiosity, wandering thru the slim, crowded lanes of Kowloon. The town's points of interest, sounds, and smells have been a kaleidoscope of reviews, every leaving an indelible imprint on his younger mind. But it wasn't all vivid lights and colourful streets. In the 1940s and Fifties, Hong Kong turned into furthermore an area of political turmoil and social unrest. It became in this environment that Bruce's early information of justice, equality, and resilience have become forged.

One of the defining moments of his youth turned into his initiation into martial arts. It wasn't a preference born out of mere hobby but a want. The young Lee positioned himself often embroiled in road fights due to the difficult community he grew up in. Concerned for his safety, his parents introduced him to Wing Chun, a style of Kung Fu, below the tutelage of the mythical Ip Man. This modified into not absolutely martial arts education; it changed into the start of a lifelong adventure in pursuit of self-expression thru physical and intellectual hassle.

Yet, Bruce's childhood changed into now not completely defined via martial arts. Thanks to his father's connections, he became also a toddler superstar within the burgeoning Hong Kong film organization. By the time he have become a teen, he had appeared in severa movies, displaying a herbal flair for overall performance. These early studies in front of the digital camera had been to play a large function in his later life, blending his martial arts skills with an innate know-how of the cinematic global.

But life in Hong Kong changed into now not without its demanding conditions. The societal constraints and limited opportunities in a positioned up-battle town set the level for the subsequent economic spoil of his life – moving to the US. This choice, driven in element through his involvement in avenue fights and the selection for a broader horizon, marked the give up of his Hong Kong youngsters and the begin of an incredible journey that might see him emerge as a global icon.

Bruce Lee's Hong Kong childhood turn out to be a crucible of kinds, forging the energy, agility, and philosophical underpinnings that would later define him. From the busy streets of Kowloon to the disciplined quiet of Ip Man's martial arts college, each experience, each venture, and each triumph carried out a element in moulding the young boy into the cultural phenomenon he have become to come to be. His early years have been a testomony to the electricity of resilience, the importance of cultural roots, and the unyielding pursuit of excellence – problems that would resonate for the duration of his existence and past.

Bruce Lee's Hong Kong have turn out to be greater than just a backdrop; it end up a person in his existence tale, colorful and pulsating with lifestyles, shaping the individual that may later captivate the arena together along along with his physical prowess, profound philosophy and indomitable spirit. This became the start of a legacy, the early brush strokes on the canvas of a existence that could encourage tens of hundreds of thousands. In the story of Bruce Lee, Hong Kong have end up not certainly an area to start; it modified into the inspiration upon which the legend modified into built.

First Foray into Acting

Bruce Lee's first foray into appearing, a course that could in the end catapult him into turning into a international icon, started out out no longer within the bustling streets of Hollywood, but within the energetic movie studios of Hong Kong. Born proper proper into a family with strong ties to the enjoyment enterprise, Bruce turn out to be exposed to performing at an early age. This revel in customary his profession and his approach to martial arts and lifestyles.

His father, Lee Hoi-Chuen, a renowned Cantonese opera massive name, have become the number one to introduce younger Bruce to the limelight. It's charming that Bruce's initial steps towards stardom had been almost unintentional. His herbal air of mystery and simplicity in front of the digicam stuck the attention of movie manufacturers inside the course of 1 in each of his father's performances. At the gentle age of three months, he debuted within the movie "Golden Gate Girl," setting the level for a series of appearances in Hong Kong cinema.

Bruce regarded in over 20 films as a infant actor, showcasing a unprecedented versatility for someone so younger. He wasn't simply some different infant celeb; he brought an infectious strength and intensity to his roles, features that could later outline his performances in martial arts cinema. Whether inside the coronary heart-wrenching drama

"The Kid" or the extra comedic "The Orphan," Bruce displayed a great functionality to connect to his target market, transcending language and cultural boundaries.

But it wasn't all easy sailing. The global of youth performing end up difficult, demanding long hours and situation which have been taxing for a boy his age. Yet, Bruce took those demanding conditions in stride, reading precious training about perseverance, tough paintings, and the artwork of average performance. These early evaluations in front of the virtual digicam honed his skills, no longer truely as an actor but as a martial artist as nicely, teaching him the significance of expression, timing, and presence.

Bruce's acting profession in Hong Kong laid the foundation for his later fulfillment in Hollywood. It have end up right here that he located out a way to captivate an target marketplace, a manner to convey emotion via motion, and the manner to inform a tale with out phrases. These abilities must show valuable as he broke into the American movie organization, wherein he needed to exhibit his martial arts prowess and triumph over cultural stereotypes and language limitations.

His early roles mixed movement and drama, reflecting the duality of his character and hobbies. In movies like "My Son, Ah Cheun" and "Infancy," he explored subject matters of own family, conflict, and resilience that resonated along together with his non-public life and philosophies. These movies have been greater than leisure; they had been a canvas upon which Bruce painted his knowledge of existence, emotion, and human connection.

Bruce's transition from a infant actor in Hong Kong to a worldwide martial arts icon in Hollywood modified into now not most effective a trade in region but a change in identification. He carried the lessons of his early performing profession, the use of them to his martial arts and philosophy. The subject, expressiveness, and ability to hook up with an purpose market that he developed as a toddler actor have end up imperative to his identity as a martial artist and an actor.

In reflecting on Bruce Lee's journey, it is apparent that his first foray into appearing became more than handiest a stepping stone; it have end up the forging of a direction that could lead him to come to be one of the maximum influential figures in each martial arts and cinema. From the studios of Hong Kong to the worldwide stage, Bruce's early performing profession modified into a vital part of his adventure, a adventure marked with the aid of the use of ardour, willpower, and an unyielding willpower to excellence. These early years within the the the front of the camera have been now not pretty lots making movies but approximately laying the foundation for a legacy that might encourage future generations.

The Street Fighter Emerges

In the labyrinthine streets of Hong Kong, amidst the hustle and din of a city pulsating with existence, a greater younger Bruce Lee started to forge his identification not really as a martial artist however as a fighter in the most correct and raw experience. This bankruptcy of his lifestyles, often much less pointed out yet crucially formative, changed into in which the street fighter inside him emerged – a aspect that could later define his method to martial arts and his philosophy of lifestyles.

Born into the placed up-battle technology, in which street gangs have been vast in Hong Kong, Bruce decided himself confronted with the cruel realities of city lifestyles at a younger age. It changed right into a global in which disputes were settled not with terms however with fists and kicks. For Bruce, those had been no longer mere road brawls; they had been instructions in survival, every come upon education him extra about himself and the paintings of fight.

Why did Bruce combat? Was it the joys, the want to assert himself, or something deeper? It may be a aggregate of a number of those factors. Bruce wasn't searching out problem however couldn't back off from a undertaking both. His participation in those avenue fights wasn't quite a bargain bodily dominance; it have become about attempting out his abilties, refining his technique, and information the psychology of combat under the maximum stressful and unpredictable situations.

These skirmishes had been greater than mere bodily confrontations; they have been a crucible that tempered his spirit. Bruce began to expand a popularity as an impressive road fighter who might also moreover need to preserve his private closer to older and larger warring parties. This recognition added each admire and problem. It solidified his reputation among his friends and made him a target for rival gangs and warring parties.

What set Bruce apart in those avenue fights wasn't truely his physical prowess however his strategic thinking. He began to look fight not simply as a physical struggle but as a chess game, in which each drift had a motive, and each motion modified proper into a reaction to an opponent's weak point. This approach modified into in its nascent tiers, but it laid the inspiration for what may also later become his philosophy of Jeet Kune Do. This martial art form emphasised adaptability, performance, and ease.

Bruce's encounters at the streets of Hong Kong additionally taught him approximately the restrictions of conventional martial arts in actual-worldwide fight. He realized that at the same time as conventional bureaucracy were adorable and steeped in statistics, they have been regularly impractical inside the unpredictable chaos of a avenue combat. This attention come to be pivotal, critical him to question and ultimately break a ways from the rigid systems of traditional martial arts.

These street stopping research additionally imbued a feel of humility and understand for his opponents in Bruce. He understood that overconfidence might be as unstable as underestimating an opponent inside the unforgiving area of street combat. This appreciate for others, regardless of their history or know-how level, have become a trademark of his character as a martial artist and person.

The transformation from a more youthful boy participating in avenue fights to a martial artist with a philosophy modified into slow however profound. Bruce's reviews on the streets of Hong Kong had been a much cry from the managed environment of a martial arts college. They were uncooked, unscripted, and unpredictable. Yet, it changed into on this chaos that he discovered clarity — readability about the character of fight, the significance of model, and the need for a martial art that turn out to be fluid, responsive, and direct.

The emergence of Bruce Lee as a road fighter changed into greater than simplest a phase; it became the forging of a warrior's spirit and the begin of a philosophy that could revolutionize martial arts. These evaluations laid the foundation for his later successes, each inside the global of martial arts and in Hollywood. They have been the beginnings of a legend, a story of a man who took the commands from the streets and grew to turn out to be them right into a legacy that keeps inspiring and featuring an impact on. The road fighter in Bruce Lee become not truly a part of his past; it come to be a important piece of the puzzle that made him the icon he is in recent times.

Chapter 2: Journey To San Francisco

The journey of Bruce Lee from the crowded streets of Hong Kong to the expansive avenues of San Francisco is a tale of ambition, cultural transition, and the start of a new financial smash in the existence of a future legend. It changed into inside the overdue Nineteen Fifties that Bruce, then a vibrant teenager complete of dreams and aspirations, made the ambitious go with the flow inside the direction of the Pacific Ocean to the us. This adventure have become now not most effective a physical relocation but a bounce proper into a destiny that would shape no longer only his destiny but additionally the world of martial arts and cinema.

Bruce became no stranger to common overall performance and spectacle. However, San Francisco supplied a starkly wonderful backdrop from the bustling film studios and colourful streets of Hong Kong. In this new international, with its severa lifestyle and possibilities, Bruce was hoping to discover the method to specific his specific abilties and philosophies.

Why San Francisco? The solution lies in part in his birthright. Bruce grow to be born in San Francisco at the same time as his father become on tour with the Cantonese opera. This truth granted him the critical right to American citizenship. This privilege changed into uncommon for lots Asians at some stage in that period. San Francisco, recognized for its massive Chinese community, promised a experience of familiarity in a remote places land, a bridge a number of the East and the West that Bruce changed into approximately to bypass.

Upon his arrival, the transition have become hard. The cultural surprise changed into apparent. Bruce navigated a international highly unique from the only he had said. He changed proper right into a teenagers caught amongst worlds, searching out his identity in a land in which he turn out to be appeared as an outsider. The preliminary days had been marked through using way of a battle to conform and in form in, to discover his vicinity in a society that turn out to be frequently unwelcoming to immigrants.

However, Bruce modified into no longer one to be deterred with the resource of adversity. His resilience, a trait honed at the streets of Hong Kong, got here to the fore as he began to locate his footing in San Francisco. He took up weird jobs, from geared up tables to education dance, each manner education him some component precious, be it humility, state of affairs, or the sheer charge of difficult art work.

One of his most sizable choices at some point of this period turn out to be to maintain his martial arts education. Bruce began education martial arts to his fellow Americans, a float which have become now not commonplace on the time. His style, but, became awesome. He changed into not just coaching techniques; he become supplying a philosophy. His technique to martial arts contemplated his tales – fluid, adaptable, and continuously evolving. This philosophy caught the attention of many, and soon, Bruce emerge as not only a martial arts trainer however a sought-after one.

In San Francisco, Bruce's views on martial arts commenced to crystallize. He noticed the restrictions of traditional martial arts in actual combat conditions. He commenced out growing a tool that became extra sensible, direct, and free from the inflexible kinds of conventional patterns. This turn out to be the begin of what may also later become Jeet Kune Do. This martial arts philosophy would likely revolutionize the way martial arts have been perceived and practiced global.

Bruce's time in San Francisco come to be a period of growth and self-discovery. He enrolled in college to have a have a observe philosophy, which profoundly delivered about his martial arts and existence philosophy. The intellectual surroundings of the college provided a modern region for Bruce to explore and question, increasing his mind and data of the sector.

This phase of Bruce's existence changed into a bridge amongst his beyond and his future. San Francisco allowed him to experiment, find out, and specific himself in approaches now not feasible in Hong Kong. Here, the suggestions of his destiny successes had been laid within the quiet moments of mirrored image, inside the rigorous education schooling, and within the regular struggles of an immigrant on the lookout for to make his mark.

Bruce's adventure to San Francisco changed into greater than a physical relocation; it changed right right into a transformative revel in. Here, the street fighter from Hong Kong commenced to morph right into a martial artist, a reality seeker, and a cultural icon. This adventure was the start of a few issue new, some detail revolutionary. It have turn out to be the begin of the legend of Bruce Lee.

Struggle and Survival in a New Land

Arriving in San Francisco inside the past due Nineteen Fifties, Lee have emerge as thrust right into a global massively particular from the best he had regarded. This new land, with its unexpected customs and language boundaries, offered many annoying situations and opportunities for growth and self-discovery.

In the ones early days, Lee's lifestyles in America balanced maintaining his cultural identity and adapting to his new environment. He decided himself amid a society that changed into once in a while unwelcoming to immigrants. The experience of being an intruder changed into palpable, and the war to find out recognition and recognize modified into a every day struggle. But Bruce Lee turn out to be not one to backtrack from a mission. His resilience, honed through his reviews within the streets of Hong Kong, have turn out to be his greatest asset.

One of the most big struggles Lee confronted became financial. Without the comfort of a strong earnings, each day turn out to be a hustle. He took on severa jobs, from prepared tables to coaching the cha-cha, a dance he had mastered in Hong Kong. These jobs, whilst humble, were instrumental in shaping his person. They taught him the fee of difficult paintings, humility, and the importance of connecting with people from all walks of existence.

But it have emerge as thru martial arts that Lee decided his true calling in this new land. He started education martial arts to his fellow Americans, a exercising that end up, on the time, quite unconventional. His approach to martial arts modified into revolutionary, emphasizing practicality over way of life. This philosophy often located him at odds with the mounted martial arts community. Yet, this method attracted severa college college students, from police officers to lawyers or maybe fellow actors.

Bruce's survival in America turn out to be no longer most effective a physical war but an intellectual and emotional one. He enrolled on the University of Washington to take a look at philosophy. This scenario profoundly stimulated his technique to martial arts and lifestyles. College life provided disturbing situations, from language barriers to balancing lecturers collectively together with his burgeoning profession as a martial arts trainer. Yet, the ones disturbing situations handiest served to deepen his remedy.

The cultural and racial limitations Lee faced have been the most daunting. In a land in which Asians had been frequently stereotyped and marginalized, he struggled to discover roles in Hollywood which have been no longer demeaning or stereotypical. This battle was now not quite tons personal fulfillment; it have turn out to be a fight for instance, for the honour of his history. Lee refused to be pigeonholed into the stereotypical roles Hollywood provided, a choice that clearly slowed his rise to fame but spoke volumes approximately his integrity and imaginative and prescient.

Lee's philosophy of Jeet Kune Do changed into born within the route of those years of war. It modified right into a martial artwork that mirrored his lifestyles stories — fluid, adaptable, and unbounded via tradition. Jeet Kune Do become greater than only a stopping style; it end up a way of lifestyles, embodying the idea that one need to be like water — adaptable, resilient, and unstoppable.

Throughout his adventure on this new land, Lee's circle of relatives grow to be a supply of power and grounding. His marriage to Linda Emery and the begin of his youngsters, Brandon and Shannon, gave him a enjoy of cause and belonging. They have been the anchor in his lifestyles, reminding him of what in reality mattered amid the chaos and annoying situations of his career.

Bruce Lee's tale in America is virtually one among triumph over adversity. It is the story of a man who, in opposition to all odds, cast a legacy that transcended martial arts and cinema. His battle and survival on this new land had been now not just about private success however about breaking boundaries, tough stereotypes, and paving the manner for destiny generations. The chapters of his life in America have been a testomony to the enduring spirit of a person who refused to be defined by means of his circumstances. This guy lived thru his non-public terms and, in doing so, have become an icon.

Philosophy and Drama

Bruce Lee's collegiate years were a length of profound growth and exploration, pivotal in shaping the man or woman and the legend he would possibly emerge as. During this time at the University of Washington, Lee delved into disciplines that deeply resonated with him: philosophy and drama. These fields of have a study were no longer truly instructional hobbies; they were avenues through which Bruce engaged with the area, burdened traditional beliefs, and honed his particular mind-set on existence and paintings.

In philosophy instructions, Bruce located himself immersed in a international of thoughts. He become particularly inquisitive about the teachings of Eastern philosophers, finding parallels among their requirements and martial arts requirements. But Bruce did not definitely soak up those teachings; he perplexed them, dissected them, and regularly debated vigorously together along with his professors and buddies. This period modified into crucial in developing his private philosophy, which later have come to be the foundation of his martial arts fashion, Jeet Kune Do. Lee's philosophy wasn't limited to the summary; it grow to be realistic, a way of existence emphasizing adaptability, simplicity, and directness.

But what end up the characteristic of drama in Bruce Lee's life in some unspecified time in the future of these collegiate years? Drama and appearing furnished a creative outlet for him to specific himself and connect with others. His involvement in the drama branch on the University of Washington grow to be approximately extra than simply getting to know the craft of appearing. It turned into about expertise human emotions, storytelling, and the energy of presence — abilties that could display precious in his later film career. Through drama, Bruce discovered to carry complex emotions and ideas via phrases, body language, and facial expressions. This potential ought to grow to be a hallmark of his everyday standard overall performance.

The interaction amongst philosophy and drama in Lee's collegiate years changed right into a dance amongst perception and expression. Philosophy provided the framework for his records of life, at the same time as drama supplied a way to particular that know-how. This synergy among belief and movement became obtrusive in how Bruce approached martial arts. His preventing style end up now not in truth bodily; it said his philosophy – fluid, adaptable, and with out useless movements.

While on the university, Bruce additionally began coaching martial arts to his fellow college students, an unconventional exercising. His instructions have been more than self-protection education; they were existence commands. He advocated his students to expect significantly, question traditional beliefs, and discover their personal direction, actually as he did in his studies.

Lee's years in university have been moreover a time of private traumatic situations and boom. He confronted financial struggles, walking severa jobs to aid himself and his schooling. He moreover professional the disturbing conditions of being an Asian in America inside the course of a time of great racial prejudice. While challenging, those research simplest reinforced his remedy and willpower to his goals.

In those collegiate years, we see the emergence of Bruce Lee no longer simply as a martial artist however as a fact seeker, a creator, and a rise up. He have become forming the center of his philosophy, a mix of Eastern and Western idea, which could later revolutionize martial arts and the way people approach life. His involvement in drama in some unspecified time in the future of this period became now not quite lots performing; it became about facts and connecting with the human enjoy, a capacity that might make him one of the most cherished and influential figures in cinema.

Bruce Lee's time on the University of Washington modified into more than a bankruptcy in his instructional life; it end up a length of transformation. The information and memories he acquired in a few unspecified time within the future of these years were instrumental in shaping his approach to martial arts, his profession in cinema, and his essential philosophy of existence. These were the years at the same time as a student of lifestyles began out to become a trainer, a film megastar, and a legend.

Chapter 3: Philosophy In The Decrease Back Of The Art

Lee have become now not excellent a martial artist; he became a truth seeker, and his technique to martial arts changed into deeply rooted in his philosophical beliefs. This particular combo of physical prowess and intellectual intensity is what set him apart and contributed extensively to his enduring legacy.

At the coronary coronary heart of Bruce Lee's philosophy became the concept of self-actualization – the concept that the remaining purpose of existence is to recognize one's whole capability. Lee believed that martial arts were a way to this end, a discipline via which one ought to acquire bodily, intellectual, and spiritual growth. His training became not just about honing the body, however additionally about hard the mind and nurturing the spirit.

Lee's creation to philosophy started out inside the route of his collegiate years on the

University of Washington, in which he delved into both Eastern and Western philosophical traditions. He end up specially inspired with the useful resource of manner of the instructions of Taoism, Buddhism, and Confucianism, which emphasized harmony, balance, and the cultivation of the inner self. These requirements have grow to be a cornerstone of his personal philosophy and drastically influenced his approach to martial arts.

One of the maximum profound necessities that Bruce Lee embraced become the Taoist principle of 'wu wei', which interprets to 'clean movement' or 'movement thru state of no activity'. This principle is ready aligning with the natural flow of lifestyles and responding to conditions with spontaneous and suitable motion. Lee included this concept into his martial arts, advocating for a style that become bendy, adaptive, and natural. This philosophy became encapsulated in his famous metaphor: "Be water, my friend. Water can waft or it may crash. Be water, my pal."

Another key problem of Lee's philosophy become the rejection of rigid styles and office work in martial arts. He believed that traditional martial arts were too constrained and did not appropriately put together practitioners for the unpredictability of actual fight. This introduced approximately the creation of Jeet Kune Do, a martial arts philosophy that emphasised simplicity, directness, and personal expression. Jeet Kune Do changed into no longer a style, but a idea that recommended human beings to discover their unique stopping approach, unencumbered with the resource of manner of the limitations of styles and paperwork.

Bruce Lee's philosophical journey have become moreover marked via the usage of his observe of Western philosophy, particularly the works of thinkers like Socrates, Plato, and Descartes. He have grow to be intrigued through their exploration of the self, reality, and knowledge, and those issue subjects frequently located expression in his writings and teachings. Lee's personal library contained an array of philosophical texts, reflecting his first-rate-ranging highbrow pursuits and his belief within the importance of persistent analyzing and self-improvement.

Lee's philosophy prolonged beyond the vicinity of martial arts. He performed those requirements to his everyday existence, striving for personal excellence in all additives. His approach to life turned into holistic – he believed inside the importance of a wholesome frame, a pointy thoughts, and a non violent spirit. His private practices blanketed regular bodily schooling, meditation, studying, and writing, all of which contributed to his improvement as a martial artist and a person.

Bruce Lee's philosophy have come to be about breaking barriers – amongst body and mind, amongst East and West, amongst art work and philosophy. He observed martial arts as a manner of existence, a course to non-public liberation and self-expression. His teachings preserve to resonate with humans across the place, now not simply as a manual to martial arts, but as a philosophy for living a big and proper lifestyles. Bruce Lee's legacy isn't surely that of a martial artist or a film movie star; it's far the legacy of a logician, a instructor, and a philosopher who showed us the art work of dwelling with cause and ardour.

Formulating a New Martial Arts Style

In the dynamic lifestyles of Bruce Lee, the method of a modern day martial arts style stands as a pivotal economic break. This have become not actually the arrival of every other martial arts gadget; it turn out to be an in depth rethinking of what martial arts could be. It turn out to be a mix of philosophy and fight, instinct and technological expertise, tradition and innovation. This new style, known as Jeet Kune Do, end up Lee's technique to the constraints he discovered in conventional martial arts and meditated his specific philosophy on life and preventing.

The origins of Jeet Kune Do, or "the manner of the intercepting fist," lay in Lee's reviews in each Hong Kong and the us. Trained in Wing Chun in Hong Kong, Bruce became exposed to a fashion that emphasized usual performance, directness, and simplicity. However, as he started out coaching martial arts in America, he determined out the regulations of sticking to at least one traditional fashion. Real combat have become unpredictable and fluid, and no single fashion want to offer solutions to each feasible situation.

Lee's technique to developing this new fashion have end up revolutionary. He believed in the principle of "the usage of no manner as manner, having no trouble as hassle." This intended that Jeet Kune Do modified into now not a hard and fast set of strategies, but a philosophy that encouraged non-stop getting to know and variation. He studied numerous martial arts paperwork which include boxing, fencing, and numerous Eastern martial arts disciplines, extracting factors that he determined effective and integrating them into his exercising.

What set Jeet Kune Do aside have end up its emphasis on practicality, normal overall performance, and flexibility. Bruce encouraged for a form of martial arts that changed into stripped of the useless, decorative moves that served more ritual than real fight. He centered on what became direct, honest, and effective. Speed, timing, and monetary system of movement were the cornerstones of Jeet Kune Do. It become about being fluid, like water, which takes the shape of its subject however can also crash with stress whilst needed.

Bruce's time in America, specifically his evaluations in Seattle and later in Oakland and Los Angeles, performed a full-size feature in the improvement of Jeet Kune Do. It turned into in those towns that he encountered opponents from numerous backgrounds and styles, every come upon assisting him refine his art work shape. His famous healthy with Wong Jack Man in Oakland changed into specially influential. The combat, which grow to be greater a warfare of philosophies than best a bodily war, led Lee to reconsider his method to martial arts, making it more dynamic and responsive.

Furthermore, Bruce Lee's involvement in films additionally inspired the improvement of Jeet Kune Do. His need to create a style that changed into not handiest effective however moreover visually compelling for the display show led him to incorporate dynamic and powerful strategies. This made Jeet Kune Do not only a martial art work, however a spectacle, a few thing that captured the creativeness of his target market.

Yet, Jeet Kune Do grow to be greater than only a preventing tool; it was a manner of questioning. It have emerge as about self-expression and private liberation. Bruce noticed simply all and sundry as a very particular man or woman and believed that each fighter should make bigger a fashion that applicable their very own bodily and highbrow developments. He encouraged his university college students to be like artists, the use of martial arts as their canvas to particular themselves truly and freely.

In developing Jeet Kune Do, Bruce Lee broke down the conventional obstacles in the international of martial arts. He challenged the norms and advocated a greater open, adaptive method to preventing and to life. Jeet Kune Do modified right into a mirrored image of his notion within the capability of the individual, the significance of self-statistics, and the fee of personal freedom.

Bruce Lee's technique of a brand new martial arts fashion grow to be greater than simplest a contribution to the world of fight; it changed into a legacy that changed how people view martial arts. It became a testament to his creativity, his philosophical intensity, and his unending pursuit of self-development. Jeet Kune Do lives on as a colorful, evolving paintings, embodying the spirit of its founder and persevering with to encourage martial artists round the arena.

Impact on Martial Arts Community

The impact of Bruce Lee on the martial arts network is a phenomenon that reverberates even a few years after his premature loss of existence. His legacy transcends the bounds of martial arts, influencing not only the techniques and philosophies inner numerous styles but also reworking the global perception of martial arts itself.

Bruce Lee emerged in a length at the same time as martial arts have been in large element enshrined in conventional practices, often locked indoors cultural and stylistic barriers. His arrival at the scene come to be like a gust of clean wind; it challenged modern-day norms and provoked a rethinking of what martial arts can be. Through his unique philosophy and method, Lee have become a current-day determine, no longer simply inside the techniques he mounted, but in his broader imaginative and prescient of what it alleged to be a martial artist.

One of the maximum large affects of Bruce Lee have end up his characteristic in popularizing martial arts within the West. Before him, martial arts had been in massive part unknown or misunderstood within the Western global. Through his films and television appearances, Lee brought the artwork shape into the dwelling rooms of hundreds of lots, captivating audiences along with his charismatic screen presence and his super bodily abilities. He become no longer handiest a fighter; he have become a performer who need to bring the beauty, agility, and energy of martial arts in a way that became reachable and exciting to a significant aim market.

However, Lee's have an effect on became not restrained to popularization. He challenged the martial arts community to conform. His philosophy of Jeet Kune Do, with its emphasis on practicality, adaptability, and private expression, was current. He encouraged martial artists to "take in what is beneficial, discard what is not, and upload what is uniquely your very own." This philosophy broke the mould of rigid, style-certain education and opened the door for skip-education and the integration of numerous martial arts patterns.

Lee's insistence on practical effectiveness in combat added approximately the incorporation of a much wider range of techniques in martial arts, which consist of elements from boxing, wrestling, and fencing. This have become a thorough departure from the norm and laid the idea for what may need to later evolve into combined martial arts (MMA). Today, MMA warring parties regularly cite Bruce Lee as a pioneer and an perception, seeing him because the first to illustrate the effectiveness of blending various preventing strategies in a cohesive method.

Another vital location where Lee's have an effect on is obvious is inside the prolonged focus on physical conditioning and power education in martial arts. Lee end up ahead of his time in his records of the location of bodily fitness in martial arts universal performance. His rigorous education regime, progressive use of gadget, and emphasis on a properly-rounded fitness recurring revolutionized how martial artists expert their our bodies. He showed that martial arts have been now not pretty an awful lot approach but furthermore about physical and intellectual conditioning.

Moreover, Lee achieved a important function in breaking racial limitations and stereotypes in the amusement industry and beyond. As an Asian actor and martial artist, he challenged the triumphing stereotypes of Asian guys in Hollywood and paved the way for future generations of actors and martial artists from various backgrounds. He became a cultural icon who used his platform to indicate for equality and example.

In the location of philosophy, Bruce Lee's teachings prolonged beyond the physical elements of martial arts. He delved into the spiritual and mental dimensions, drawing on various Eastern and Western philosophies. His method turned into holistic, viewing martial arts as a way of lifestyles that encompasses bodily, intellectual, and religious well-being. His teachings preserve to encourage martial artists around the arena, encouraging them to view martial arts as a journey of personal and religious increase.

Bruce Lee's effect on the martial arts community is immeasurable. He revolutionized martial arts education, broke cultural limitations, and left a legacy that keeps encouraging and evolving. His imaginative and prescient and philosophy transcended the boundaries of martial arts, leaving a lasting imprint now not simplest at the art shape itself but moreover at the broader cultural panorama. Bruce Lee turn out to be extra than a martial artist; he became a visionary who changed the manner the area considered martial arts, all of the time.

Chapter 4: The Green Hornet Kato Rises

The journey of Bruce Lee from a passionate martial artist to a global icon took a large bounce beforehand together together with his feature as Kato in "The Green Hornet." This duration of his life emerge as now not best a career milestone; it was a cultural phenomenon that could all the time exchange the panorama of each television and martial arts.

In the mid-Sixties, "The Green Hornet," a tv show primarily based on a radio series of the identical name, have end up the platform that delivered Bruce Lee to American audiences. Cast as Kato, the sidekick to the titular character, Lee have emerge as to begin with visible as a secondary decide within the show. However, it wasn't prolonged before his top notch abilties and screen presence caught the eye of traffic at a few stage inside the USA and beyond.

Bruce Lee's portrayal of Kato comes to be groundbreaking in lots of techniques. At a time whilst Asian actors in Hollywood were regularly relegated to stereotypical roles, Lee's Kato became a character of substance and potential. He wasn't simply the hero's assistant; he have become a powerful pressure in his very personal proper. With his easy black gown and iconic mask, Kato have turn out to be a photograph of favor, electricity, and agility.

One of the maximum big contributions of Bruce Lee in "The Green Hornet" have become the advent of actual martial arts to mainstream American tv. Before Lee, martial arts were in large part misrepresented or overly dramatized in Western media. As Kato, Bruce added authenticity and depth to the fight scenes that were previously unseen. His fluidity, velocity, and precision in martial arts no longer best mesmerized the audience but moreover raised the bar for motion choreography in tv and cinema.

The effect of Bruce Lee's portrayal of Kato prolonged beyond the boundaries of the show. It challenged the triumphing stereotypes and perceptions of Asians in Western media. Kato come to be now not a clichéd character; he changed into a hero in his private right, resonating with audiences across racial and cultural divides. Lee's average performance opened doorways for greater various and real representations of Asians in Hollywood.

"The Green Hornet" moreover served as a platform for Lee to expose off his philosophy of martial arts. In each episode, Lee infused Kato with a revel in of grace, performance, and purpose - requirements that he deeply believed in. His movement sequences have been more than just entertainment; they have been an expression of his martial arts ideology, emphasizing adaptability, directness, and simplicity.

Moreover, the show have become a stepping stone that propelled Bruce Lee to worldwide reputation. While "The Green Hornet" cherished mild achievement inside the United States, it modified into a massive hit in Hong Kong, incomes Lee a cult following. This popularity in his area of start would possibly later open doorways to a a success profession in Hong Kong cinema, primary to his iconic films that revolutionized the martial arts style.

Behind the scenes, Bruce Lee modified into a perfectionist, constantly pushing the limits of what is probably finished in motion sequences. His dedication to the craft and his insistence on authenticity introduced a brand new degree of credibility to martial arts in amusement. He professional carefully for the function, and his self-discipline to excellence have become obtrusive in every go with the flow he made on show show.

"The Green Hornet" was extra than handiest a tv show for Bruce Lee; it modified proper right into a catalyst that ignited his career and set him on the course to becoming a legend. As Kato, Lee left an indelible mark no longer only at the martial arts network however additionally on famous tradition. His legacy in the show lives on, inspiring generations of martial artists and actors, and persevering with to captivate audiences round the world.

"The Green Hornet: Kato Rises" is not excellent a bankruptcy in Bruce Lee's biography; it's far a testament to his capabilities, vision, and enduring effect on the arena of entertainment and martial arts. Through his portrayal of Kato, Bruce Lee rose from being a expert martial artist to a cultural icon, all the time converting the way the location sees martial arts and Asian actors in Hollywood.

Challenges in a Biased Industry

Bruce Lee's ascent inside the entertainment company became a protracted manner from a easy adventure; it was riddled with stressful conditions, many stemming from the biases and stereotypes huge in Hollywood on the time. His reviews in this biased company were now not simply private hurdles however moreover reflections of the broader struggles faced with the resource of manner of Asian artists in the West.

When Lee arrived in Hollywood, the movie agency have turn out to be steeped in a way of life that rarely afforded big opportunities to Asian actors. They were frequently relegated to roles which have been stereotypical and demeaning, a far cry from the main hero kinds that Lee aspired to portray. The commercial enterprise organization's narrow angle on race and casting saw Asian characters generally portrayed with the beneficial useful resource of Western actors in 'yellowface,' similarly marginalizing actual Asian actors.

For Lee, one of the first massive traumatic situations come to be breaking thru those racial limitations. Despite his easy air of mystery and abilities, he determined himself restricted to roles which have been confined in depth and scope. His first foremost break in Hollywood, as Kato in "The Green Hornet," irrespective of the fact that groundbreaking, moreover underscored this stereotyping. The function, even as massive, although strong him because the sidekick to a Western hero. Lee's aspirations to be a top guy have been constantly met with resistance, a reflected picture of the organization's reluctance to veer a protracted way from its entrenched racial biases.

Bruce Lee's warfare in Hollywood have grow to be not quite tons getting roles; it turned into approximately changing the narrative spherical Asian characters. He sought to painting Asian characters with depth, dignity, and electricity, countering the accepted stereotypes. This quest become met with resistance from studio executives and casting administrators who regularly couldn't see beyond the mounted norms. Lee's imaginative and prescient for a cutting-edge form of Asian individual in Western cinema end up revolutionary however tough for masses in the commercial enterprise organisation to accept.

Furthermore, Lee's particular fashion of martial arts changed into often misunderstood in the West. While he favored to show off right martial arts, Hollywood grow to be aware about a greater stylized, exaggerated form of on-display screen preventing. His insistence on realism and effectiveness in fight scenes modified right into a departure from the norm and required him to continuously advocate for his approach.

Despite the ones stressful situations, Bruce Lee's resilience and resolution in no way wavered. He constantly labored on enhancing his craft, every as a martial artist and an actor. His philosophy of adapting to circumstances served him nicely as he navigated the complexities of Hollywood. Lee started out out growing his very very own possibilities, writing and pitching movie mind that might show off his imaginative and prescient of martial arts and Asian characters.

Lee's staying strength commenced out to pay off, albeit slowly. His skills and on-display presence have been plain, and slowly, the organization commenced to take be aware. However, his biggest breakthroughs came not in Hollywood, but in Hong Kong cinema. Frustrated with the constrained opportunities in Hollywood, Lee again to Hong Kong, in which he modified into met with immense recognition. His movies made in Hong Kong, at the side of "The Big Boss" and "Fist of Fury," have been big successes and in the end gave him the modern freedom and leading roles he had lengthy sought.

The irony of Bruce Lee's adventure in the leisure corporation is that his success in Hong Kong would circle lower lower back to influence Hollywood. His worldwide reputation and the global fulfillment of his films in the end broke down obstacles in Hollywood, paving the manner for additonal diverse and respectful representations of Asian characters.

Bruce Lee's challenges within the biased Hollywood enterprise had been emblematic of a larger struggle in the direction of racial stereotypes and constrained instance. His perseverance and imaginative and prescient not high-quality helped him overcome the ones disturbing situations but moreover laid the groundwork for future generations of actors and filmmakers. Lee's legacy within the film enterprise goes beyond his roles and his films; it lies in his relentless combat in competition to bias, his reshaping of Asian illustration in cinema, and his breaking of cultural obstacles that had long been unchallenged in Hollywood.

The Path to Stardom

Bruce Lee's direction to stardom have become a journey marked thru perseverance, innovation, and an unyielding determination to his craft. From the crowded streets of Hong Kong to the smooth avenues of Hollywood, his journey have become not pretty much turning into a celebrity but about revolutionizing the region of martial arts and cinema.

Lee's early years in Hong Kong, in which he have grow to be born to a circle of relatives of performers, laid the inspiration for his later achievement. He regarded in numerous films as a little one actor, which gave him an early flavor of the film organisation. However, the confines of the Hong Kong movie enterprise could not include his ambition, predominant him to America – a land of opportunity but also of task.

In the united states, Lee faced a cultural landscape that come to be in massive component unaccommodating to Asian actors. Despite the limitations, his strength of mind did not waver. He commenced coaching martial arts in Seattle, in which his innovative technique to combat and charismatic education style fast obtained him a following. His philosophy, which emphasised adaptability and self-expression, have become no longer definitely confined to martial arts but permeated his complete technique to existence and in the end his performing.

Lee's damage in Hollywood came with "The Green Hornet," in which he finished Kato, the crime-stopping accomplice of the titular individual. While the function become groundbreaking, it additionally stereotyped him as a sidekick. However, Lee's portrayal of Kato became magnetic, displaying his martial arts prowess and on-display display display screen air of mystery. The show have grow to be a stepping stone, introducing him to a miles broader American audience and showcasing his precise abilties.

Chapter 5: Making Of A Martial Arts Classic

The advent of martial arts conventional thru Bruce Lee is a story of vision, innovation, and cultural effect. His journey to redefine the fashion is a story of an artist who now not handiest excelled in his craft however moreover converted it, leaving an indelible mark at the arena of cinema and martial arts.

Bruce Lee's method to creating martial arts traditional began collectively with his philosophy. He believed in an proper instance of martial arts, one which modified into grounded in practicality and realism His frustration with the exaggerated depictions commonly visible in movies at the time end up the catalyst for his innovative technique. He wanted to showcase martial arts now not without a doubt as a spectacle but as a paintings shape that come to be every stunning and lethal, a real instance of the ability and region it required.

The manner of creating a martial arts traditional concerned meticulous making plans and innovation Lee's interest to detail turn out to be now not confined to the combat choreography; it extended to every element of production – from the storyline and individual improvement to the cinematography and modifying. He changed into deeply worried inside the scriptwriting technique, ensuring that the narrative changed into compelling and that it seamlessly blanketed the martial arts sequences.

In the choreography of the fight scenes, Lee's genius really shone. He choreographed sequences that had been realistic but visually adorable, breaking a long manner from the conventional mould of martial arts films. His actions have been fluid and specific, each strike and block telling a tale of its non-public. He emphasised pace, energy, and approach, making each combat scene a dance of controlled aggression and artistry.

One of Lee's most huge contributions to the making of a martial arts traditional become his emphasis on realism. He brought strategies from severa martial arts patterns, blending them to create a cutting-edge, dynamic form of on-display show display screen preventing. His use of realistic sound outcomes, near-up pix, and the portrayal of the physical toll of fight added a degree of authenticity formerly unseen in martial arts movies.

Lee's power of will to his craft prolonged to his physical training for the roles. He underwent rigorous training, pushing his frame to its limits to advantage the physicality required for his person. His awesome fitness diploma and agility introduced an extra layer of believability to his combat scenes, fascinating the target audience along together with his prowess.

Moreover, Lee emerge as a pioneer in pass-cultural cinema. He desired to create films that transcended cultural and geographical limitations, appealing to a global target market. He integrated elements from every Eastern and Western cinema, making his movies relatable to a diverse target market. His air of mystery and capability to hold deep emotions through his characters made him a cherished determine international.

The effect of Bruce Lee's martial arts classics have grow to be profound. He not high-quality changed the way martial arts had been depicted in movies however additionally prompted the worldwide belief of Asian culture and cinema. His movies broke discipline workplace statistics and opened the doors for destiny martial arts movies and stars. They stimulated generations of filmmakers and martial artists, placing a cutting-edge well-known for movement cinema.

In growing a martial arts traditional, Bruce Lee did extra than sincerely entertain; he knowledgeable. He added the art of martial arts to the main aspect, showcasing its intensity, beauty, and complexity. He broke racial barriers and stereotypes, paving the way for Asian actors in Hollywood. His legacy within the making of martial arts classics isn't always just about the films he left inside the back of; it's miles approximately the cultural shift he initiated, the muse he furnished to limitless human beings, and the art shape he advanced to new heights.

Bruce Lee's adventure in making a martial arts traditional have become a fusion of ardour, creativity, and steady pursuit of excellence. His artwork stood as a testomony to his belief in the functionality of martial arts cinema to be a actual shape of revolutionary expression. Through his classics, he left a long-lasting legacy that keeps to persuade and encourage, making him not best a famous individual of his time but a timeless icon within the worldwide of martial arts and cinema.

Cultural Impact and Reception

Bruce Lee's cultural impact and reception amplify an extended manner past his recognition as a martial arts icon and movie celebrity. His have an impact on permeated numerous components of global tradition, reshaping now not best how martial arts were perceived however moreover changing the landscape of film, breaking down racial obstacles, and inspiring philosophical discourse.

From the streets of Hong Kong to the bustling avenues of Hollywood, Lee's journey come to be marked with the useful resource of a continuing pursuit of excellence and a quest to undertaking and redefine cultural norms. His rise to stardom in the 1960s and Nineteen Seventies befell inside the route of a duration of amazing social and cultural alternate, and he emerged as a picture of this change.

In the location of cinema, Lee revolutionized the motion style. Prior to his emergence, martial arts in films were frequently portrayed in an exaggerated, nearly fantastical manner. Lee added realism and depth to martial arts choreography that become grounded in his personal rigorous training and philosophical ideals. His approach to filmmaking combined raw physicality with an emotional depth, making his characters relatable and his combat scenes a mixture of artistry and realism. This exchange no longer amazing precipitated a era of filmmakers and actors however also altered goal market expectancies for movement cinema.

Moreover, Lee's impact on the martial arts community changed into profound. He changed into instrumental in popularizing martial arts inside the West, introducing techniques and philosophies previously unknown to many outside of Asia. His philosophy of Jeet Kune Do, emphasizing adaptability, simplicity, and private expression, resonated with martial artists worldwide, influencing severa martial arts patterns and practices.

Perhaps one in all Lee's most enduring impacts turned into breaking down racial and cultural limitations. As a Chinese actor in Hollywood, he faced a panorama rife with stereotyping and discrimination. Despite the ones challenges, he refused to be typecast, combating for and growing roles that rejected the ones stereotypes. His success paved the way for destiny generations of Asian actors and multiplied the instance of Asian cultures in mainstream Western media.

Lee's cultural impact moreover extended to his off-show character. His interviews and writings decided out someone deeply engaged with philosophical questions about self-expression, non-public identification, and the character of martial arts. His thoughts, often infused with information from every Eastern and Western philosophical traditions, captivated a worldwide purpose marketplace, influencing not simplest martial artists but humans from all walks of life.

The reception to Bruce Lee's lifestyles and work became as various as it emerge as massive. In the West, he have become a symbol of bodily prowess and cinematic innovation, on the equal time as in Asia, he changed into celebrated as a cultural icon who accelerated the global stature of Asian cinema. His untimely death excellent amplified his legend, with lovers worldwide mourning the shortage of a discern who had grow to be an awful lot extra than handiest a movie superstar.

Furthermore, Lee's impact prolonged into regions likes health and self-help, collectively together together with his determination to bodily conditioning and intellectual location inspiring countless people in their non-public health trips. His writings and teachings on self-actualization and personal improvement stay referenced in motivational contexts.

Bruce Lee's cultural effect and reception are a testament to his multifaceted legacy. He modified into a trailblazer who transcended the bounds of movie and martial arts to emerge as a cultural icon. His philosophy, films, and martial arts legacy maintain to encourage and resonate with human beings around the arena, making him now not first-rate a determine of his time, but a undying image of cultural alternate and human potential.

Behind-the-Scenes Struggles

Bruce Lee's meteoric upward push to stardom turn out to be no longer with out its sincere percentage of within the returned of-the-scenes struggles. These demanding situations, in massive element unseen via the general public, ordinary his person, honed his treatment, and propelled him to redefine the limits of martial arts and cinema. Lee's tale behind the curtains is one in every of resilience, innovation, and an unyielding pursuit of his vision.

Bruce Lee end up added to the arena of show agency at a totally more youthful age, manner to his father's acting profession. However, the glitz and glamour of the movie company did little to protect him from the difficult realities of existence. His early years in Hong Kong had been marked thru the turbulence of submit-struggle existence, coupled with the hardships of residing in a crowded metropolis. These opinions instilled in him a durability and avenue-smart mind-set that could later define his approach to life and martial arts.

Lee's go back to america as a teen changed into fraught with cultural and economic worrying situations. Struggling to fit right into a society that became hugely wonderful from what he had stated in Hong Kong, he encountered racial prejudice and cultural isolation. Financial constraints further complicated his existence, compelling him to absorb numerous jobs while pursuing his schooling. These studies, at the identical time as hard, have been instrumental in shaping his philosophical outlook, deeply influencing his approach to martial arts and his preference to interrupt down racial obstacles.

In Hollywood, Lee confronted an corporation reluctance to just accept an Asian actor in leading roles. His auditions often brought approximately unhappiness, with roles being restrained to stereotypical depictions of Asian characters. This systemic bias in Hollywood no longer only restrained his performing possibilities however moreover challenged his imaginative and prescient of bringing real martial arts to mainstream cinema. Lee's response to the ones rejections have become not one of defeat but of willpower. He commenced out coaching martial arts to Hollywood stars, the usage of this as a platform to expose off his precise skills and philosophical technique to martial arts.

Lee's struggles prolonged to the producing of his films. His insistence on authenticity in martial arts choreography frequently clashed with the conventional technique of filmmakers. He confronted resistance in convincing administrators and manufacturers of the want for realistic fight scenes, which he believed have been important to the storytelling. His perfectionism and unorthodox strategies once in a while brought about conflicts on set, but they had been a testomony to his determination to excellence.

Behind the scenes, Lee changed into moreover a committed family man. Balancing his professional desires together together together with his non-public existence became a normal war. The starting of his kids brought a brand new duration to his existence, bringing pleasure however additionally new responsibilities. His partner, Linda Lee Cadwell, finished a pivotal function in supporting his career and coping with the demanding situations that got here collectively alongside with his growing recognition.

Furthermore, Lee's relentless schooling ordinary and quest for physical perfection took a toll on his frame. He driven himself to the boundaries, regularly education for hours on end to advantage the very top notch diploma of bodily health. This immoderate dedication, while contributing to his onscreen presence and martial arts prowess, moreover delivered about accidents and physical strain, exacerbating the annoying situations he faced.

Despite these in the lower back of-the-scenes struggles, Lee's spirit remained unbroken. He continued to innovate, mixing extraordinary martial arts patterns to create Jeet Kune Do, a mirrored picture of his belief in adaptability and private expression. His training, movies, and philosophy continued to garner interest, slowly breaking down the limits he confronted in the industry.

Chapter 6: Bruce Lee's Martial Arts Philosophy

Bruce Lee's martial arts philosophy, transcending mere bodily fight, modified into a synthesis of profound religious beliefs, rigorous area, and a groundbreaking technique to self-safety. Lee's philosophy come to be now not limited to the walls of traditional martial arts; it emerge as a fluid, dynamic stress that revolutionized how martial arts have been perceived and practiced global.

Bruce Lee changed into added to the arena of martial arts at a younger age. His preliminary training in Wing Chun, under the tutelage of the legendary Ip Man, laid the foundation for his future explorations in martial arts. However, it have come to be his relentless quest for self-improvement and his unorthodox thinking that led him to increase a brand new martial arts philosophy: Jeet Kune Do (The Way of the Intercepting Fist).

At the middle of Lee's martial arts philosophy have end up the idea of "the use of no way as way; having no trouble as trouble." This idea represented a great departure from conventional martial arts, which often adhered strictly to set up office work and strategies. Lee believed that those traditional paperwork were too inflexible and could not efficiently adapt to the chaos and unpredictability of real fight. His approach changed into approximately being fluid, adaptable, and open to learning from all martial arts bureaucracy.

Lee's Jeet Kune Do grow to be not virtually a set of strategies but a philosophy of lifestyles. He emphasised the importance of personal expression in fight, advocating for a martial arts style that end up unique to each individual. According to Lee, the final motive of martial arts come to be self-knowledge, and he regularly likened the exercising of martial arts to a shape of self-discovery. He recommended martial artists to "be like water," adapting to any state of affairs with out being positive through way of rigid systems.

Physical fitness and conditioning had been furthermore critical elements of Lee's martial arts philosophy. He became a pioneer in integrating diverse styles of physical training, collectively with weight education, aerobic physical sports, or maybe dance, into his routine. Lee's physical conditioning changed into no longer quite much constructing strength or patience; it modified into about growing a frame that become rapid, agile, and able to executing complicated techniques with precision and electricity.

Moreover, Lee's philosophy prolonged past the physical factors of martial arts to embody a intellectual and spiritual size. He drew concept from severa philosophical and spiritual traditions, in conjunction with Taoism, Buddhism, and Western philosophy. His writings and teachings regularly contemplated those affects, that specialize in problems which includes the individual of fact, private liberation, and the relationship among thoughts and frame.

Lee's progressive technique to martial arts moreover addressed realistic self-protection. He believed within the effectiveness of easy, direct techniques and emphasized the significance of pace, timing, and financial machine of movement. His approach have become approximately practicality and performance, stripping away any useless movements or bureaucracy that did not make a contribution to the effectiveness of the martial artist.

In the location of teaching, Bruce Lee end up a reputable determine. His technique of steering changed into incredibly custom designed, and tailored to the desires and talents of his college students. He modified into appeared for his ability to encourage and inspire, pushing his college college students to their limits on the equal time as additionally instilling in them a deep respect for the art of martial arts.

Bruce Lee's martial arts philosophy became a mirrored image of his broader vision for a greater open, adaptable, and private approach to self-protection and self-expression. It challenged the conventions of conventional martial arts and had a profound impact on martial arts communities international. His teachings hold to inspire martial artists from severa disciplines, cementing his legacy as a cutting-edge thinker and practitioner in the global of martial arts.

Training the Stars

Bruce Lee's affect extended beyond the limits of conventional martial arts into the glamorous worldwide of Hollywood, in which he have become a sought-after instructor for plenty film stars. His journey of "Training the Stars" is a fascinating economic disaster in his life, showcasing his unique capabilities, philosophies, and the profound impact he had on the ones he taught.

In the 1960s, whilst Bruce Lee moved to the us, he started out teaching martial arts in

Seattle in advance than relocating to Oakland and in the long run settling in Los Angeles. It changed into proper right here that his reputation as an extraordinary martial artist and teacher commenced to draw the attention of Hollywood's elite. Lee's philosophy and technique to martial arts have been modern, and his capability to bring the ones necessities made him an excellent trainer.

One of the key elements of Lee's training habitual emerge as his emphasis on practicality and effectiveness. He believed that martial arts ought to no longer honestly be about forms and traditions, however approximately actual-international applicability. This method appealed to actors who were searching for to carry out their personal stunts or to characteristic a layer of authenticity to their roles.

Among his most exceptional college college students had been film stars like Steve McQueen, James Coburn, and Roman

Polanski. Lee's training durations with those stars have been now not quite lots training them martial arts but also about assisting them recognize and encompass the physicality required for his or her roles. He centered on improving their agility, coordination, and interest — competencies that had been valuable for on-display performances.

Steve McQueen, frequently hailed because the "King of Cool," modified into especially inquisitive about Lee's philosophy. McQueen, regarded for his love of fast automobiles and motorcycles, located a similar thrill in martial arts education. Under Lee's steerage, McQueen honed his capabilities, which delivered an side to his on-display presence.

James Coburn, every different iconic actor of the time, modified into deeply inspired with the aid of manner of Lee's teachings. Coburn have end up curious about the religious difficulty of martial arts, and his durations with Lee went past physical training. They regularly concerned discussions about life, philosophy, and the deeper this means that inside the once more of martial arts techniques.

Lee's education durations have been immoderate and traumatic. He predicted a immoderate stage of willpower and hassle from his university university college students, competencies he embodied himself. His education techniques have been beforehand in their time, incorporating factors of electricity training, aerobic, and flexibility sporting occasions — a holistic approach that become unusual in martial arts training at the time.

Moreover, Lee's have an effect on on his college students transcended the physical problem of education. He instilled in them a sense of self notion and a latest attitude on their bodily competencies. His teachings in self-reputation and mindfulness had an extended-lasting impact on their lives, each on and rancid the show display screen.

Lee's courting collectively with his movie megastar university college college students emerge as at the same time beneficial. While they located out the artwork of martial arts and self-defense, Lee won a deeper knowledge of the film enterprise. This experience end up profitable whilst he began his non-public journey in filmmaking. The interactions together together with his college college students furnished him with insights into performing and film production, which later helped him in his transition from a martial arts instructor to a international film famous individual.

Bruce Lee's function in "Training the Stars" grow to be a testament to his versatility as a martial artist and an educator. He changed into no longer only a instructor however moreover a mentor and an concept to many in Hollywood. Through his modern training techniques and philosophical teachings, he left an extended-lasting impact on his college students, lots of whom went directly to include what they decided from him into their expert and personal lives. Bruce Lee's legacy in education Hollywood stars is a fascinating problem of his super existence story, reflecting his effect no longer certainly as a martial artist, but as a cultural icon that bridged the distance among East and West.

Influence on Modern Martial Arts

Bruce Lee's have an effect on on modern martial arts is notable, transcending time and geographical barriers. His progressive technique, charismatic personality, and philosophical insights revolutionized no longer simply martial arts but additionally how they may be perceived globally. This profound impact has etched his legacy into the annals of martial arts statistics, making him a respected figure lengthy after his premature loss of lifestyles.

Bruce Lee became raised in Hong Kong, wherein he emerge as introduced to the sector of martial arts. His early schooling started out out with Wing Chun, under the tutelage of Yip Man, but Lee's unquenchable thirst for knowledge and development led him to discover numerous notable styles. This exploration have become the seed from which his later progressive thoughts sprouted.

Lee's flow into to the us in his overdue young adults marked the begin of a modern-day financial smash. In the U.S., he started out teaching martial arts, first of all to his fellow college students and later to a broader target market in Seattle, Oakland, and Los Angeles. It grow to be in the direction of this era that the principles of his influential philosophy, Jeet Kune Do, were laid.

Jeet Kune Do, or "The Way of the Intercepting Fist," grow to be Bruce Lee's technique to what he observed because the anxiety and impracticality of traditional martial arts. It modified right into a philosophy that emphasised adaptability, performance, and simplicity. Lee believed in a martial arts idea that have end up unfastened from the confines of styles and patterns. He endorsed for a form of martial arts that become fluid and aware of the dynamics of real fight.

One of the important issue factors of Lee's affect on present day-day martial arts become his emphasis on actual-international utility. He insisted that martial arts ought to be sensible and powerful in actual self-safety situations. This pragmatism became a giant shift from the extra conventional types of martial arts, which regularly targeted on ceremonial elements or rigid, predetermined gadgets of moves.

Lee's schooling recurring and strategies had been modern-day-day. He protected components from diverse martial arts disciplines and even from one-of-a-kind types of physical conditioning together with weight training, cardiovascular sporting activities, or maybe dance. This holistic technique to education not only greater the bodily talents required for martial arts but furthermore broadened the scope of what schooling need to encompass.

Moreover, Bruce Lee became a pioneer in selling the integration of the highbrow and philosophical additives into martial arts. He turned into deeply stimulated by way of manner of Taoist and Zen philosophy, which he seamlessly wove into his teachings and exercising. His famous adage, "Be water, my buddy," encapsulates this philosophy — the concept of being bendy and adaptable in each fight and existence.

Lee's have an effect on prolonged past the sector of martial arts into the wider cultural sphere through his movie career. His films, which embody "Enter the Dragon," "The Way of the Dragon," and "Fist of Fury," introduced martial arts to an worldwide goal market and sparked a worldwide hobby in Asian martial arts. He became one of the first to demonstrate the capability of martial arts in cinematic storytelling, integrating thrilling combat scenes with compelling narratives.

His portrayal of martial artists in his films furthermore helped shatter longstanding stereotypes. He supplied the martial artist as a robust, principled, and multifaceted person, countering the frequently one-dimensional portrayal of Asian characters in Hollywood at the time. This no longer handiest opened doors for future Asian actors and martial artists in Hollywood but moreover advanced the reputation of martial arts to a reputable artwork form.

In the arena of martial arts, Bruce Lee's have an impact on is seen in the massive adoption of circulate-education and a extra open-minded approach to excellent stopping patterns. Modern mixed martial arts (MMA) owes plenty to Lee's philosophy of taking what's beneficial from various martial arts office work and combining them into a cohesive, effective combating fashion. He is often referred to as the daddy of MMA, a testomony to his lasting have an effect on.

Bruce Lee's impact on present day-day martial arts is indelible. He converted martial arts from a inflexible, style-positive trouble right proper right into a dynamic, adaptable form of self-expression. His teachings preserve to resonate with martial artists and fanatics global, inspiring them to technique martial arts now not honestly as a physical pursuit, however as a way of existence. Lee's legacy in martial arts isn't always clearly about the bodily techniques he brought or the films he starred in; it's far approximately the enduring philosophy he imparted and the manner he stimulated human beings to count on in every other manner approximately the paintings of combat and the art work of dwelling.

Chapter 7: Meeting Linda Lee

Bruce Lee's meeting with Linda Emery, who would possibly later become Linda Lee Cadwell, marked a pivotal bankruptcy in his lifestyles, intertwining a personal love story collectively together along with his journey as a martial artist and cultural icon. Their union turn out to be no longer handiest a merging of hearts; it have become a fusion of cultures, ideals, and goals that performed a substantial role in Bruce's existence and legacy.

In the early 1960s, Bruce Lee changed into making his mark in Seattle, education martial arts and studying philosophy at the University of Washington. It have come to be proper right here, amidst his growing reputation as a professional martial artist and charismatic teacher, that he met Linda Emery, a young scholar interested by martial arts. Linda, a excessive university pupil at the time, modified into inquisitive about Lee's martial arts school with the useful resource of manner of his growing popularity.

From the start, their connection modified into undeniable. Linda modified into captivated thru Bruce's passion for martial arts, his depth, and his philosophical outlook on existence. For Bruce, Linda represented now not most effective a loving companion however also a bridge among his Eastern history and the Western world he become navigating. Their courting blossomed amidst a backdrop of societal norms that often considered interracial relationships with skepticism and prejudice.

Despite those societal challenges, their bond simplest grew stronger. They shared commonplace values and goals, with Linda embracing Bruce's objectives and supporting his aspirations. In 1964, in reality years once they met, Bruce and Linda decided to solidify their commitment to every extraordinary and were given married in a smooth ceremony in Seattle. This union marked the beginning of a partnership that might extensively effect Bruce's private and professional life.

Linda's assist modified into unwavering as Bruce pursued his dream of popularizing martial arts internationally. She end up through his side as he confronted the traumatic situations of breaking into Hollywood, a journey fraught with racial obstacles and stereotyping. Linda's notion in Bruce's know-how and imaginative and prescient supplied him with a sturdy emotional basis, allowing him to navigate the unpredictable waters of reputation and cultural affect.

Together, Bruce and Linda commenced a own family, welcoming their son Brandon in 1965 and their daughter Shannon in 1969. Family lifestyles have come to be a supply of pleasure and grounding for Bruce, who emerge as deeply committed to being a loving father and husband. Linda's function in their family went past that of a partner and mom; she have become an essential a part of Bruce's adventure, dealing with his career and assisting him installation his martial arts faculties.

The interracial nature of Bruce and Linda's marriage at some stage in the 1960s and Seventies become emblematic of the societal changes taking area in the United States. Their dating stood as a testomony to the energy of love overcoming cultural and racial barriers, reflecting the converting attitudes in the direction of race and marriage.

Linda's position in Bruce's existence extended past his untimely lack of life in 1973 She have become the custodian of his legacy, making sure that his philosophies, teachings, and the essence of his paintings had been because it should be preserved and shared with the arena. She authored numerous books about Bruce, supplying insights into his lifestyles, beliefs, and the profound effect he had as a martial artist, actor, and cultural icon.

The assembly of Bruce and Linda Lee turn out to be greater than a romantic tale; it modified right right into a union that deeply triggered the route of Bruce's lifestyles and artwork. Linda's unwavering assist, knowledge, and love accomplished a important feature in Bruce's journey, allowing him to pursue his dreams with the guarantee that he changed into now not on my own. Together, they navigated the complexities of life, leaving a legacy that continues to encourage and resonate with humans at a few degree in the globe.

Balancing Fame and Family

In the whirlwind of Bruce Lee's tremendous life, one of the maximum tough additives he confronted became balancing the needs of burgeoning repute collectively collectively together with his deep dedication to circle of relatives. This part of Lee's journey offers a glimpse into his individual beyond the public person, revealing a person who valued the sanctity of his private lifestyles and the well-being of his loved ones.

Bruce Lee's ascent to stardom become rapid and excessive. Following his breakout feature as Kato in "The Green Hornet" and subsequent success in Hong Kong cinema, he speedy became an international sensation. With this popularity got here the relentless needs of his profession - rigorous education schedules, prolonged hours on set, public appearances, and the pressures of being in the limelight. Yet, amidst this nerve-racking tempo, Lee have become a devoted family guy, deeply connected to his partner, Linda, and their children, Brandon and Shannon.

Lee's marriage to Linda Emery in 1964 modified proper right into a huge turning point in his life. Linda became now not most effective a accomplice but a pillar of help, coping with the realistic components in their lifestyles together at the equal time as also offering emotional grounding. Their relationship changed into based on mutual recognize and know-how, with Linda embracing the cultural nuances of Lee's historic past and supporting his ambitious career goals.

The delivery in their son Brandon in 1965 and daughter Shannon in 1969 introduced new dimensions of pleasure and duty to Lee's life. He cherished his feature as a father, endeavoring to spend amazing time along with his kids irrespective of his busy time table. Lee grow to be diagnosed to bring his own family to film gadgets, integrating his non-public and professional worlds. He desired his kids to apprehend and admire his artwork, hoping to instill in them the identical passion for martial arts and the humanities he cherished.

However, balancing recognition and circle of relatives modified into no longer with out its demanding situations. The wishes of his profession regularly meant lengthy intervals faraway from home, taxing both Lee and his circle of relatives. The bodily toll of his excessive training and movie schedules, coupled with the strain of constant media interest, additionally affected his fitness and personal existence. Lee become acutely privy to those pressures and strived to maintain a healthful paintings-life stability, often turning to his philosophical ideals for guidance and attitude.

Lee's philosophy, intently stimulated by means of Taoism and Buddhism, emphasized harmony and balance, principles he tried to use in his personal lifestyles. He believed within the significance of personal nicely-being, data that his potential to be an first rate husband and father have come to be intrinsically connected to his bodily and highbrow fitness. This philosophy guided him in making selections that aligned alongside collectively with his values, even supposing they conflicted with professional possibilities.

Moreover, Lee's rise to reputation coincided with a period of excessive cultural and social exchange globally. His interracial marriage and global success made his family lifestyles a subject of public hobby, which he navigated with grace and dignity. Lee and Linda's courting stood as a testomony to their love and dedication within the face of societal norms and prejudices.

Throughout his lifestyles, Lee became someone pushed with the useful resource of first rate ambition and a relentless paintings ethic. Yet, his letters, interviews, and interactions with close to friends and own family painted the image of someone for whom own family come to be a sanctuary, a supply of satisfaction, and a grounding stress. He often cited the importance of affection, know-how, and the simple pleasures of existence with own family.

Bruce Lee's capability to balance reputation and own family is a lesser-seemed however fundamental a part of his story. It famous a multidimensional person who navigated the complexities of an incredible lifestyles with a deep experience of duty toward his cherished ones. His devotion to his own family amidst the whirlwind of reputation modified into as an lousy lot part of his legacy as his groundbreaking achievements in martial arts and cinema. Bruce Lee's lifestyles, consequently, is not simplest a tale of a cultural icon but a story of someone striving to find equilibrium in a existence full of first rate needs and profound love.

Fatherhood

The function of fatherhood in Bruce Lee's life have become taken into consideration considered one of profound importance, together with a layer of intensity and cause to his extremely good adventure. While the arena knew him as a martial arts icon and a film star, to his youngsters, Brandon and Shannon, he have come to be surely 'Dad' - a characteristic he cherished deeply and prioritized amidst his bustling existence.

Born proper right into a global of stardom and martial arts, Bruce Lee's kids were delivered early to their father's specific life-style. Lee, who have become a father for the number one time with the delivery of Brandon in 1965, and again with Shannon in 1969, embraced fatherhood with the equal depth and passion he added to his expert lifestyles. However, in evaluation to his public man or woman, Lee's method to parenting emerge as marked via a smooth, nurturing, and thoughtful presence.

Lee's philosophy on martial arts and existence deeply precipitated his parenting style. He considered fatherhood not simply as a responsibility however as an possibility to impart information and values to his children. He believed in leading with the useful resource of example, instilling in Brandon and Shannon the significance of region, admire, and the pursuit of excellence. Lee's teachings to his youngsters often transcended martial arts, delving into the geographical areas of philosophy, self-expression, and the importance of dwelling a existence with cause.

Despite his traumatic career, Lee have become a palms-on father. He took an energetic position within the upbringing of his kids, frequently visible gambling with them, schooling them, and associated with them in his daily ordinary. His schooling classes now and again doubled as playtime, with Brandon and Shannon eagerly searching or perhaps taking aspect. This integration of his expert and private lifestyles modified into Lee's manner of balancing his responsibilities at the equal time as ensuring his youngsters were a part of his international.

Lee's technique to fatherhood turned into moreover coloured by using using the use of his own upbringing and cultural history. He valued the classes he observed out from his parents and sought to pass on similar values, which embody recognize for elders, the importance of family, and a robust artwork ethic. At the same time, Lee, who had expert the demanding conditions of being raised in cultures, changed into keenly privy to giving his kids a experience of belonging and identification.

As a father, Lee changed into moreover shielding and deeply involved approximately the welfare of his kids. He desired to guard them from the pitfalls of recognition and the general public eye, striving to provide them with a normal upbringing notwithstanding his developing celebrity popularity. Lee's surprising and untimely death in 1973 changed into a devastating blow to his young circle of relatives, leaving a void that became deeply felt. However, the requirements and love he instilled in his children remained as guiding forces of their lives.

Linda Lee Cadwell, Bruce's spouse, carried out an instrumental feature in retaining his memory and teachings alive for their kids. She ensured that Brandon and Shannon grew up data their father's legacy, now not actually as a martial artist and actor but as a person with deep philosophical insights and a boundless love for his circle of relatives.

Fatherhood turned into a applicable, defining detail of Bruce Lee's life. It modified into a role he carried out with delight, strength of thoughts, and love. His technique to parenting comes to be a mirrored image of his broader philosophical beliefs and a testomony to his individual. For Bruce Lee, his satisfactory legacy became not his films or his martial arts prowess, but the values and classes he exceeded without delay to his youngsters, shaping their lives and ensuring that his spirit lived on via them.

Chapter 8: Roots In San Francisco

A Glimpse into the Lee Family

Every remarkable existence is strong inside the crucible of family, and Bruce Lee's early years were no exception. The tale of Bruce Lee begins off evolved alongside together with his mother and father, Lee Hoi-chuen and Grace Ho. His father, Lee Hoi-chuen, have become a Cantonese opera superstar, a person who reveled in the limelight of the Chinese theater. But lifestyles within the theater wasn't without its hardships, and the Lee circle of relatives regularly decided themselves on the circulate, chasing performances and the ephemeral applause of the aim market.

Grace Ho, Bruce's mother, changed into herself a girl of exquisite man or woman. Of Eurasian descent, Grace delivered a touch of range to the Lee circle of relatives. She have become the bridge amongst worlds, a picture of the multicultural tapestry that would come to outline each Bruce and San Francisco itself.

The Multicultural Tapestry of San Francisco

San Francisco within the 1940s emerges as a city at the crossroads of cultures. The Bay City has turn out to be a melting pot, a place in which unique ethnicities and traditions converged. For Bruce Lee, growing up on this form of numerous surroundings might shape his outlook on existence in profound approaches.

In San Francisco's Chinatown, wherein the Lee circle of relatives settled, younger Bruce become uncovered to a wealthy array of cultural impacts. The narrow streets, decorated with the bright crimson and gold of Chinese lanterns, have come to be his playground. The tantalizing aroma of Chinese cuisine wafted through the air, whilst the cacophony of distant places languages supplied a symphony of sounds.

But for Bruce, the cultural mosaic come to be no longer limited to in fact one network. San Francisco became a microcosm of the place, and he have become keenly aware of the opportunities it presented. The proximity of severa communities exposed him to not incredible Chinese traditions however moreover the influences of the West. It become a town that endorsed the embrace of numerous cultures, an area in which boundaries blurred, and the opportunities for a younger boy had been as countless as the horizon.

Bruce Lee's Birth and Early Years

On November 27, 1940, in San Francisco's Chinatown, Bruce Jun Fan Lee got here into the area. From his earliest days, it became obvious that he become a little one of remarkable electricity and charisma. A photo of the East and the West, Bruce's combined ancient past become a mirrored image of his birthplace – a metropolis that celebrated variety.

His early years have been marked thru manner of a precocious nature and an insatiable hobby. The younger Bruce come to be a mischievous, colorful presence inside the

Lee family. His mother and father, in their ceaseless pursuit of their goals, identified their son's boundless functionality. They nurtured his spirit and recommended his pastimes, laying the muse for a destiny legend.

The Impact of a Vibrant Chinatown

The vibrancy of Chinatown modified into greater than a backdrop for Bruce's teenagers; it modified into a defining pressure. In the coronary heart of San Francisco's Chinese community, he witnessed the relentless pursuit of dreams and the unyielding spirit of folks who sought to break loose from societal constraints. The hustle and bustle of this specific community furnished an schooling that couldn't be decided in the walls of a study room.

But it end up additionally a community with its percentage of traumatic situations. For a sensitive more youthful boy like Bruce, the streets of Chinatown held each wonder and, at times, trouble. He confronted bullying and taunting from his friends, a crucible of man or woman that might shape his resilient spirit.

In Bruce's early years, the teeming streets of Chinatown served as his first martial arts academy, an area wherein he placed out to preserve his own. His early memories with adversity set the degree for a existence defined with the aid of the pursuit of excellence, as he launched right into a adventure that would take him from those colorful streets to international stardom.

The more youthful Bruce Lee's existence, packed with the colours and contrasts of San Francisco's multicultural landscape, set the degree for a future in evaluation to a few different. The Lee family's journey turns out to be a testament to the boundless opportunities of the American Dream, and Bruce's birthplace, with its wealthy tapestry of cultures, laid the foundation for his future as a international icon. This have become the begin of a tale that would embody no longer nice a personal tale of battle and triumph but moreover the cultural transformation of an technology.

Chapter 9: Early Challenges And Influences

The Bullying and Alienation

Bruce Lee's journey into the world of martial arts grow to be no longer truly one in every of mere desire; it turn out to be born out of necessity. In the tumultuous landscape of his children, the younger Bruce confronted adversaries that might form the trajectory of his lifestyles. San Francisco, with its various tapestry, grow to be a place of possibility, however it have emerge as moreover a breeding ground for prejudice and discrimination.

As a infant of blended historical beyond, Bruce was a target for bullies. The cruelty he continued on the streets of San Francisco modified into a crucible that examined his resilience. Yet, even in the face of adversity, Bruce refused to go into opposite. His early years taught him that worry and humiliation have been not the future he expected for himself.

The bullying and alienation he skilled have been catalysts for change. They ignited a fire inner him, propelling him inside the route of the path of martial arts as a way of self-safety and self-discovery. It end up within the depths of his early struggles that the seed of his martial ambition end up planted.

Kung Fu Beginnings with Yip Man

Bruce's salvation got here even as his father, Lee Hoi-chuen, recognizing his son's want for guidance and problem, added him to Yip Man, a renowned martial artist who taught the Wing Chun fashion of kung fu. Yip Man have become now not only Bruce's instructor but additionally his mentor and father discern. Under the guidance of Yip Man, Bruce commenced out to domesticate not only his bodily prowess however moreover his indomitable spirit.

The rigorous schooling in Wing Chun turn out to be a formative experience for Bruce. It instilled in him the ideas of financial system of motion, directness, and simplicity that could later emerge as the cornerstones of his martial philosophy. Yip Man's teachings, grounded in way of lifestyles however open to innovation, left an indelible mark on the more youthful Bruce Lee.

It have turn out to be in some unspecified time in the destiny of this period that Bruce evolved an insatiable urge for meals for know-how. He voraciously devoured books on martial arts and philosophy, delving deep into the standards that could form his future pastimes. The seed of his martial ambition commenced to sprout as he honed his abilities and immersed himself within the worldwide of kung fu.

Hong Kong: A Formative Experience

Bruce's journey took a amazing flip at the same time as, at the age of 13, he moved to Hong Kong along together together with his family. This relocation marked a pivotal 2nd in his existence, wherein he might go through a profound transformation. Hong Kong, with its bustling streets, changed into a miles cry from the multicultural landscape of San Francisco. It became a town teeming with life, power, and manner of life, in which historic traditions intertwined with modernity.

In Hong Kong, Bruce come to be uncovered to a broader spectrum of martial arts, beyond the confines of Wing Chun. He started to discover severa disciplines, absorbing strategies from considered one of a kind patterns and traditions. This period of exploration allowed him to forge his direction, to extract what emerge as useful and discard what emerge as no longer, a principle that might later define his martial philosophy.

His time in Hong Kong became marked no longer incredible with the useful resource of martial discovery however furthermore via manner of manner of a revel in of belonging. It modified into right right here that Bruce started out to installation a call for himself within the nearby martial arts network. His growing capability and recognition as a powerful fighter set the extent for his return to the us, where he may similarly carve his very private identity inside the global of martial arts.

The Seed of Martial Ambition

The early disturbing conditions and impacts in Bruce Lee's existence sowed the seeds of a high-quality ambition. They had been the crucible wherein he cast his indomitable will, a crucible that converted a bullied younger boy proper right into a martial arts legend.

Bruce's opinions with bullying and alienation fueled his choice for self-improvement and resilience. Yip Man's mentorship and the training of Wing Chun instilled in him the center ideas of martial arts. And the colourful streets of Hong Kong provided the fertile floor for his exploration of numerous martial disciplines.

Chapter 10: Martial Arts Odyssey

Gung Fu: The Martial Philosophy

In the annals of martial arts, one call sticks out particularly others—Bruce Lee. The name is synonymous with a philosophy, a manner of life, and an technique to combat that transcends the limits of time and tradition. At the coronary coronary heart of this legacy lies the concept of "Gung Fu," a term frequently spelled as "Kung Fu." However, for Bruce Lee, it changed into greater than only a preventing style; it become a martial philosophy that have end up the cornerstone of his life's art work.

Gung Fu, which means "knowledge carried out through difficult paintings," end up not quite a whole lot learning a fixed of techniques however become a direction to self-discovery, self-development, and ultimately self-expression. Bruce believed that proper Gung Fu changed into no longer sure thru any specific machine or lifestyle however turned into a continuously evolving adventure of private boom. It turned into the muse upon which he must assemble his martial philosophy, Jeet Kune Do.

The idea of Gung Fu have come to be no longer restrained to martial arts by myself; it have end up a manner of thinking, a way of drawing near lifestyles itself. It turn out to be approximately stripping away the superfluous, attending to the essence of things, and adapting to the ever-changing situations of life. It changed into in this philosophy that Bruce Lee located no longer best his motive however additionally a completely unique voice that would resonate with humans at some stage in the globe.

Seattle's Wing Luke Museum

Bruce Lee's lifestyles come to be a tapestry woven with threads from special cultures and traditions, and in 1959, the metropolis of Seattle have grow to be the backdrop for the subsequent financial disaster in his martial arts adventure. It have end up right right here that he should start to introduce the world to the profound and multifaceted philosophy of Gung Fu.

Seattle became now not most effective the metropolis in which he could in all likelihood deepen his statistics of martial arts however moreover the place wherein he could plant the seeds of his innovation. Among the maximum big influences sooner or later of this era grow to be his creation to the neighborhood Wing Luke Museum, a place in which he would possibly delve deeper into his Chinese ancient past and the roots of martial arts.

Bruce's exploration of the museum's famous and artifacts unearthed the information and cultural context of Chinese martial arts, improving his knowledge of the wealthy way of lifestyles he become inheriting. It changed proper right into a period of introspection, as he sought to hook up with his historic past and reconcile it with the ever-evolving philosophy he was growing.

Seattle's Wing Luke Museum provided the historical foundation upon which Bruce Lee ought to assemble a cutting-edge martial philosophy. He diagnosed that to innovate, one want to understand and admire the past. It changed into here that he began out to forge a extra profound connection some of the historic traditions of the East and his imaginative and prescient of a global martial art work.

The Lure of Martial Arts: Jun Fan Gung Fu

Bruce Lee's tireless pursuit of martial information led him to the installed order of Jun Fan Gung Fu, a machine that bore his Chinese call, Jun Fan. Jun Fan Gung Fu come to be a manifestation of his martial philosophy, a fusion of techniques and ideas drawn from diverse martial arts, emphasizing practicality, overall performance, and directness.

It modified into an artwork that refused to be confined by means of way of the inflexible systems of lifestyle. Instead, Jun Fan Gung Fu embraced the principle of edition and evolution, embodying the essence of Bruce's Gung Fu philosophy. His imaginative and prescient modified into to create a fashion that end up not without a doubt a set of strategies however a manner of life, an method to self-discovery, and an avenue for non-public growth.

Bruce Lee's introduction of Jun Fan Gung Fu marked the beginning of a modern day technology in martial arts. It grow to be a testomony to his notion that one want to absorb what's beneficial and discard what isn't always, a principle that might later grow to be the middle of his mythical martial philosophy, Jeet Kune Do. Jun Fan Gung Fu became a prelude to a extra revolution in martial arts, one that would inspire generations to go back.

Martial Arts Exploration: Beyond Wing Chun

Bruce Lee's journey changed into considered one among ceaseless exploration, an odyssey into the coronary coronary heart of martial arts itself. The conventional form of Wing Chun, which he had positioned out under Yip Man, end up best the begin. Bruce modified into no longer content material fabric to live within the limitations of a single style; he yearned to increase his horizons and assimilate the simplest factors from outstanding martial arts disciplines.

His quest took him to locations as diverse because the streets of Seattle and the mountain areas of Hong Kong, in which he sought out legendary martial artists and challenged himself in techniques that few dared. From Muay Thai to Western boxing, from fencing to grappling, Bruce's relentless pursuit of information led him to head past the regulations of any single system.

As he delved deeper into the area of martial arts, Bruce Lee's vision grew broader. He discovered out that the vital component to powerful combat have become no longer adhering to a fixed of rigid strategies however expertise the ideas that underpinned all martial arts. This profound notion laid the muse for his groundbreaking martial philosophy, Jeet Kune Do, that can come to represent the pinnacle of martial innovation.

The Road to Hollywood

Family Relocation to America

The direction to greatness is frequently marked with the resource of twists and turns, and Bruce Lee's journey have become no exception. In the Fifties, the Lee circle of relatives, accompanied via a more youthful Bruce, made a enormous choice that would ultimately set the volume for his exquisite career. They left the colourful streets of Hong Kong and released into a modern-day journey thru transferring to the USA.

For Bruce, the glide to America have emerge as a defining moment. It modified into a transition from the conventional and culturally rich backdrop of Hong Kong to the land of possibility, a place wherein he need to have the hazard to carve his course. The skip represented an impressive leap into the unknown, and it modified into during this period that Bruce's indomitable spirit absolutely commenced out to emerge.

Seattle: Setting the Stage

The Lee own family settled within the city of Seattle, Washington, an area wherein possibilities and stressful conditions awaited them. It grow to be in Seattle that the more youthful Bruce can also take his first steps on the street to turning into a worldwide icon. The metropolis's rich cultural variety supplied fertile floor for a younger guy keen to discover his very own identity.

Seattle set the degree for Bruce's adventure, no longer best as a martial artist however moreover as a philosopher and a reality seeker. The city's colourful combo of cultures and traditions supplied a unique mind-set that might deeply have an effect on Bruce's private and intellectual increase. It changed into right right right here that he first commenced out out to grapple with questions of identification, belonging, and cause.

The University Years

Bruce's quest for understanding changed into insatiable. His time in Seattle led him to the University of Washington, wherein he pursued a diploma in philosophy. It grow to be at some stage in his university years that he started out to meld the philosophical necessities of the East with the analytical and vital considering the West.

His research in philosophy not best prolonged his intellectual horizons but moreover knowledgeable his martial arts philosophy. Bruce Lee's philosophy became now not pretty much physical combat; it modified right into a holistic approach to life itself. It turn out to be a belief that one's non-public increase and development must be a regular, evolving method. His time at the university helped him refine the ones mind and lay the intellectual foundation for what have to later become Jeet Kune Do.

Kato on "The Green Hornet"

Bruce Lee's journey into Hollywood became marked via manner of energy of thoughts and tenacity. His arrival in America, coupled together with his developing recognition as a martial artist and his precise philosophical attitude, opened doors within the entertainment industry. It wasn't long in advance than Bruce made his first vast foray into the world of performing.

In 1966, Bruce Lee turn out to be solid in a characteristic that might set the diploma for his Hollywood career: Kato within the television collection "The Green Hornet." Kato come to be no longer just a sidekick however a man or woman who showcased Bruce's tremendous martial abilities. The feature catapulted him into the American public's cognizance and have grow to be a cultural touchstone.

As Kato, Bruce Lee have end up a sensation, leaving an indelible mark on the sector of tv. His explosive air of mystery and incredible martial artistry drew in audiences, and the display's reputation soared. Bruce had bridged cultures, introducing the arena to a modern-day type of motion hero, one which transcended racial stereotypes and redefined the notion of a sidekick.

Early Achievements and Challenges

Despite the fulfillment of "The Green Hornet," Bruce Lee confronted annoying situations that lay earlier. The street to stardom changed into now not without its bumps and hurdles. His unyielding spirit and resilience had been tested in the pretty competitive global of Hollywood.

While his feature as Kato introduced him popularity, it additionally left him grappling with the regulations of the roles to be had to Asian actors on the time. Bruce Lee, however, modified into not one to be restricted via stereotypes or conventions. He diagnosed the want for exchange, now not simplest for himself however for the endless folks who would probably come after him.

His early achievements and challenges in Hollywood laid the groundwork for a extra undertaking. Bruce Lee modified into decided to interrupt through those limitations, redefine the jobs of Asian actors, and go away a long lasting legacy that could circulate past the silver show.

Breaking Hollywood Barriers

The Challenge of Stereotyping

Bruce Lee's journey thru the labyrinth of Hollywood changed into a testament to his unwavering self-discipline to go past the confines of racial stereotyping. In an corporation in which Asian actors have been regularly relegated to caricatured roles and marginalized to the outer fringe of the silver show, Bruce Lee determined an opportunity no longer handiest for himself but for future generations. He diagnosed the want to interrupt unfastened from those stifling molds and redefine the Asian photograph within the worldwide of amusement.

The task of stereotyping modified into not honestly a progressive one; it emerge as a moral and social vital. Bruce understood that exchange can also want to handiest come through representation, and he come to be determined to change the narrative. He launched into a assignment to shatter the ones dangerous stereotypes, a challenge that could come to be a defining subject matter in his Hollywood profession.

"The Wrecking Crew" and Bruce's Fight Scenes

In 1968, Bruce Lee's foray into Hollywood deepened when he emerge as strong inside the movie "The Wrecking Crew." It emerge as in this film that Bruce's exceptional martial arts capabilities have been showcased in a manner that had in no way been visible before on the silver show display screen. As an uncredited stunt double, he choreographed and completed a fight scene that left audiences in awe.

"The Wrecking Crew" marked a turning element in Bruce Lee's career. It became a testament to his capabilities and the potential for martial arts to captivate audiences. His extremely good physical prowess and outstanding agility set a new favored for motion sequences, setting the stage for what was to go back.

The film's fight scene became mythical, a precursor to Bruce's future as an motion icon. It changed right into a image of his determination to interrupt loose from the restrictions of stereotyping, showing that Asian actors will be extra than surely sidekicks or villains. Bruce had taken step one in the direction of altering Hollywood's belief of martial artists and Asian actors.

Bruce Lee's Vision: Breaking Stereotypes

Bruce Lee's imaginative and prescient became not restricted to his career; it have become a visionary quest to adjust the very cloth of Hollywood's tapestry. He understood the want of converting perceptions and the effect it may have on society. He anticipated a global wherein Asian characters might be portrayed with depth, complexity, and authenticity.

Bruce Lee's commitment to breaking stereotypes prolonged beyond the jobs he executed. He actively engaged with Hollywood executives, advocating for trade inside the enterprise's portrayal of Asian characters. He used his platform to push for additonal correct and respectful depictions, disturbing that the corporation understand the knowledge and capability in the Asian community.

He changed into a trailblazer, unapologetically confronting the racial limitations that permeated Hollywood. His vision become a beacon for all aspiring Asian actors, and his self-control to shatter stereotypes left an indelible mark at the leisure employer.

Hollywood's Slow Transformation

Bruce Lee's challenge to interrupt stereotypes changed into now not with out its disturbing conditions. While his effect on the sector of martial arts have become simple, the transformation of Hollywood have become a gradual method. The organization's deeply ingrained prejudices couldn't be overturned overnight. Bruce faced resistance and skepticism from dad and mom who've been hesitant to embody exchange.

It may want to take time for Hollywood to really understand the importance of his imaginative and prescient. Nevertheless, Bruce Lee's unyielding spirit and the authenticity he introduced to his roles started out to chip away on the stereotypes that had held sway for goodbye. Slowly but in fact, the panorama of Hollywood started to shift, with more possibilities starting up for Asian actors.

The seeds Bruce had sown in Hollywood's fertile floor should in the long run endure fruit, inspiring a present day technology of Asian actors and reshaping the way the arena considered Asian characters on show. His legacy have become not simply one in every of movement and martial arts, but a legacy of trade, transformation, and the relentless pursuit of justice and equality.

Chapter 11: Enter The Dragon

The Evolution of Bruce Lee's Film Career

Bruce Lee's adventure in Hollywood changed right right into a tapestry of tough-fought battles and the breaking of barriers. The traumatic situations of racial stereotyping had been palpable, but Bruce's unyielding spirit and vision were unwavering. His career in cinema end up a regular evolution, a continuing quest to redefine not most effective the Asian picture in Hollywood however moreover the very essence of movement and martial arts at the silver show.

Before "Enter the Dragon," Bruce had made big strides in the global of movie, including his iconic position as Kato in "The Green Hornet" and the unforgettable combat scene in "The Wrecking Crew." Each of those achievements contributed to the transformation of his profession. It have become obvious that Bruce become greater than just an actor; he turn out to be a trailblazer, a visionary who sought to shatter conventions and open new doorways for Asian actors in Hollywood.

Writing and Filming "Enter the Dragon"

In 1973, Bruce Lee embarked on what ought to come to be his magnum opus, "Enter the Dragon." The movie have become a groundbreaking enterprise, a challenge that could encapsulate his martial philosophy and propel him into the stratosphere of world stardom.

Bruce now not quality starred within the film however furthermore contributed to its script and choreography. It changed right into a labor of love, a testomony to his strength of will to his craft. "Enter the Dragon" come to be a hobby of his vision, a film that could not quality entertain however additionally educate. It changed right into a vehicle for Bruce to speak the intensity and knowledge of martial arts and philosophy to the sector.

The movie's manufacturing turn out to be now not with out its demanding conditions, which encompass the ever-gift anxiety among Hollywood's life-style and Bruce's imaginative and prescient of authenticity. He fought to maintain the cultural integrity of the film, making sure that it represented not best a martial arts spectacle however a actual exploration of Eastern philosophy and Western movement.

"Enter the Dragon" have emerge as a hard paintings of love and a masterpiece of storytelling. It modified proper right into a fusion of East and West, a bridge amongst cultures, and an embodiment of Bruce's quest to break the limitations of prejudice and stereotypes.

The Cultural Impact of the Film

"Enter the Dragon" have become extra than only a film; it have become a cultural phenomenon. Released in 1973, it broke new floor in the global of martial arts cinema. Bruce Lee's notable martial talents, coupled with the movie's revolutionary motion sequences, set a contemporary considerable for the genre. It showcased a stage of authenticity and pride that captivated audiences round the vicinity.

The film's fulfillment have come to be now not constrained to the vicinity of movement; it modified right into a transcendent enjoy that resonated with audiences of all backgrounds. "Enter the Dragon" represented a cultural trade, a 2d in history while the East and West got here together in party of martial arts and philosophy. It have come to be a mirrored photograph of the converting times, a international that became hungry for the sort of hero Bruce Lee had become.

The effect of the movie prolonged some distance beyond the field administrative center. It ignited a worldwide fascination with martial arts and heralded a brand new generation in Hollywood. Bruce Lee's philosophy, as depicted inside the movie, began out to permeate famous culture, influencing the entirety from style to music. "Enter the Dragon" created a seismic shift inside the worldwide of enjoyment and brought a modern-day paradigm of motion and example.

Bruce Lee's Global Stardom

"Enter the Dragon" catapulted Bruce Lee to a point of stardom that transcended the bounds of nationality. He have end up a worldwide icon, respected and celebrated from the streets of Los Angeles to the bustling towns of Asia. The effect of the film modified into immeasurable, and Bruce's popularity soared to superb heights.

His imaginative and prescient had come to fruition. He had damaged loose from the regulations of racial stereotyping and redefined the photograph of the Asian actor in Hollywood. Bruce Lee turn out to be now not just a martial artist or actor; he become a cultural ambassador, a symbol of energy, philosophy, and authenticity.

The global had in no way visible a determine quite like Bruce Lee. He became not absolutely an movement hero however a truth seeker, a instructor, and an propose for exchange. His stardom turn out to be a testament to his message, a message that went some distance past the confines of the silver show. Bruce Lee had grow to be a photograph of wish and transformation, a bridge between cultures, and a beacon of concept for generations to go back.

Jeet Kune Do: The Way of the Intercepting Fist

The Birth of a Martial Philosophy

Bruce Lee modified into now not content material material with certainly being a martial arts icon and Hollywood movie star. He aspired to depart an extended-lasting legacy, one which transcended the confines of film and recognition. It end up inside the pursuit of this profound mission that he birthed the philosophy of Jeet Kune Do, which he often called the "Way of the Intercepting Fist."

Jeet Kune Do became more than most effective a stopping style; it have become a mirrored image of Bruce's center ideals about martial arts, life, and personal boom. It grow to be a philosophy that emphasised adaptability, directness, and simplicity, ideas he had explored for the reason that his days analyzing Wing Chun with Yip Man and his academic hobbies in philosophy on the University of Washington.

The beginning of Jeet Kune Do represented the culmination of Bruce's evaluations, information, and vision. It changed right into a philosophy solid via a life-time of dedication to martial arts and self-improvement. Bruce have grow to be adamant that martial arts need to now not make sure via way of inflexible paperwork and traditions however have to be a living, evolving expression of individuality and effectiveness.

The Principles of Jeet Kune Do

Jeet Kune Do have end up described via the usage of a set of fundamental requirements that embodied Bruce Lee's specific martial philosophy. At its center, it have come to be about intercepting an opponent's attack, the use of the least quantity of attempt to advantage maximum consequences, and being unfastened from the limitations of any unique device.

One of the important thing ideas of Jeet Kune Do have turn out to be the concept of "financial system of movement." Bruce believed in minimizing wasted attempt, focusing at the maximum direct and green techniques. He emphasized simplicity, arguing that complexity in martial arts great caused confusion and ineffectiveness.

Another critical detail become the precept of "simultaneous attack and safety." Bruce promoted the idea of intercepting an opponent's attack at the same time as countering with one's actions. This approach embodied his philosophy of practicality and performance, thinking about speedy responses in fight.

Furthermore, Jeet Kune Do embraced the idea of "personal freedom." Bruce believed that each character's expression of martial arts want to be a reflected picture of their specific strengths and talents. It turned into a philosophy that recommended self-discovery and adaptability, empowering people to discover their way in martial arts and lifestyles.

Spreading the Message: Bruce Lee's Writings

Bruce Lee come to be now not content material to hold the standards of Jeet Kune Do to himself. He modified into an avid writer and philosopher, and he used his literary abilties to spread his martial philosophy to a worldwide target audience. His essays, books, and articles have become a platform for sharing his mind on martial arts, self-improvement, and personal increase.

One of his most massive works become "The Tao of Jeet Kune Do," a e-book that encapsulated the essence of his martial philosophy. It served as a guide for practitioners and enthusiasts, providing insights into the principles of Jeet Kune Do and Bruce's particular method to martial arts. The e-book stays a traditional in the international of martial arts literature, inspiring generations of martial artists and thinkers.

Through his writings, Bruce Lee encouraged human beings to impeach manner of lifestyles, searching for their course, and constantly adapt and evolve. He challenged the reputation quo, urging human beings to loose themselves from the constraints of dogma and discover their manner in martial arts and life.

The Influence of Jeet Kune Do

The effect of Jeet Kune Do extended a protracted manner beyond the arena of martial arts. Bruce Lee's philosophy resonated with people attempting to find self-improvement, non-public boom, and the pursuit of excellence. His message modified into no longer constrained to combat but have end up a blueprint for living a greater fulfilled and proper existence.

Jeet Kune Do have grow to be a catalyst for alternate within the martial arts global. It inspired a modern day technology of practitioners who embraced its ideas of adaptability, directness, and simplicity. Martial artists around the globe started out to consist of philosophy into their schooling and education, perpetuating Bruce Lee's legacy.

Moreover, the have an effect on of Jeet Kune Do reached into specific geographical regions of well-known manner of lifestyles, consisting of movie, tune, and fashion. Bruce Lee's philosophy, coupled alongside collectively together with his charismatic presence, became a cultural stress. It had the electricity to interrupt down racial limitations and redefine the photograph of the Asian actor in Hollywood. He have end up now not only a martial artist; he become a cultural icon who challenged conventions and inspired change.

Chapter 12: The Private Bruce Lee

Bruce Lee's Complex Personality

Beyond the cinematic legend and martial arts icon lay a man of complicated and multifaceted individual. Bruce Lee changed into greater than simply the sum of his achievements; he grow to be a person who grappled with a myriad of emotions, aspirations, and contradictions.

He have become acknowledged for his intense consciousness, unwavering strength of mind, and boundless energy. His self-control to his craft turn out to be unrivaled, and his commitment to breaking racial stereotypes emerge as determined. Yet, underneath the charismatic and confident out of doors have become a personal guy who wrestled with insecurities, doubts, and the relentless pursuit of perfection.

Bruce Lee's persona changed into a paradox. On one hand, he became exuberant and charismatic, drawing humans to him along along with his infectious enthusiasm. On the possibility hand, he have become deeply introspective, often out of area in idea as he pondered the mysteries of lifestyles and the man or woman of existence.

Family Life and Fatherhood

Amidst the glitz and glamour of his Hollywood career, Bruce Lee loved his circle of relatives lifestyles. His marriage to Linda Emery and the begin of his two children, Brandon and Shannon, were assets of giant pleasure and success. It became within the confines of his own family that he determined solace and love, a ways removed from the pressures and expectations of stardom.

As a father, Bruce become dedicated and demanding, instilling in his youngsters the values of difficult art work, discipline, and recognize. He became determined to be a gift and guiding decide in their lives, but the traumatic nature of his profession.

The tragic loss of his son, Brandon, in a shooting twist of destiny end up a devastating blow that Bruce Lee and Linda needed to go through. It become a length of profound grief and mirrored picture, one which tested the electricity of their own family bonds. It grow to be at some point of those times that Bruce's personal persona, marked via introspection and resilience, shone thru.

A Perpetual Quest for Self-Improvement

Bruce Lee's pursuit of self-improvement extended beyond the martial arts arena. He changed into a voracious reader and a deep thinker, delving into philosophy, psychology, and personal improvement. His library come to be full of volumes on a numerous kind of topics, from Eastern philosophy to Western psychology.

He believed that one's quest for excellence ought to be all-encompassing, extending to each component of life. Bruce became a proponent of personal boom and self-actualization, continuously striving to be the high-quality model of himself. He understood that proper mastery became now not limited to physical abilities but extended to the thoughts and spirit.

This perpetual quest for self-development became a contemplated picture of Bruce Lee's pressured spirit. He was someone who believed within the ability for endless growth and the energy of private transformation. His personal research and reflections were the crucible in which his philosophy and martial arts superior.

The Inner Struggles

Bruce Lee's internal struggles had been an vital part of his private worldwide. The pursuit of excellence grow to be no longer with out its stressful situations. He grappled with a continuing preference for perfection and frequently felt the load of expectancies, each self-imposed and outdoor.

He emerge as acutely aware about the pressures that got here together along with his popularity and the load of being a cultural trailblazer. The burden of breaking racial stereotypes and the wishes of being a global icon weighed carefully on his shoulders. He come to be devoted to shattering conventions and redefining the Asian photograph in Hollywood, but the adventure became fraught with traumatic situations and internal conflicts.

Bruce Lee's private worldwide changed proper into a realm of introspection and self-discovery. It emerge as a place in which he sought to recognize the complexities of his man or woman and the mysteries of existence. His inner struggles were now not really battles with outdoor forces but moreover quests to recognize the depths of his soul.

Tumultuous Relationships

Love and Marriage

In the existence of Bruce Lee, relationships have been as tumultuous as the adventure of his fists and philosophy. The man who had fought to interrupt the stereotypes of

Hollywood have become not impervious to the complexities of human emotions. Love, for Bruce Lee, became each a supply of pleasure and turmoil, a testomony to the duality that often characterizes profound connections.

Before Linda Emery got here into his life, Bruce Lee had professional love and heartache in his nearby Hong Kong. His extra younger dalliances and early romantic pursuits would probably form the man or woman he changed into to come to be. But it modified into in Seattle, in which he changed into pursuing his training and martial arts journey, that he might meet Linda Emery, a kindred spirit who could in the long run turn out to be his spouse.

Their love have emerge as a profound connection, one which transcended the limits of subculture and distance. Bruce and Linda's relationship may grow to be a cornerstone of his existence, a supply of assist, love, and stability amidst the whirlwind of his Hollywood career.

Bruce Lee's Relationship with Linda

Bruce and Linda's courting turn out to be marked thru a deep bond, a shared willpower to their circle of relatives, and a partnership built on love and recognize. Linda have become now not just a dedicated partner but moreover a pillar of energy for Bruce for the duration of the difficult times in his profession.

She supported his vision, his philosophy, and his quest to break racial stereotypes in Hollywood. Linda, like Bruce, modified proper right into a truth seeker and a writer, and he or she or he or he contributed to his literary works, assisting to spread his philosophy and vision to a broader target market.

Their dating turn out to be a testomony to the long-lasting energy of love and partnership, presenting Bruce with the emotional basis to face the trials and tribulations that lay in advance.

The Marital Challenges

While Bruce and Linda's love modified into undeniable, their marriage modified into not with out its disturbing conditions. The dreams of Bruce's Hollywood career, coupled together together with his relentless quest for perfection, regularly took a toll on their dating. The pressures of fame, blended alongside along with his excessive work ethic, at instances left Linda feeling as if she have been in the shadow of his worldwide stardom.

The couple confronted financial troubles, in particular inside the early years of their marriage, which introduced strain to their dating. The struggles of an up-and-coming actor in Hollywood were exacerbated through the limited opportunities for Asian actors inside the agency at the time.

Their love modified into examined further by way of using the tragic loss of their son, Brandon, in a taking pics twist of fate. It changed right right into a profound and devastating blow that delivered their own family to the brink of melancholy. The tragedy no longer best shook their marriage however furthermore challenged the very foundations of their lives.

Personal Triumphs and Tragedies

Despite the challenges, Bruce Lee's dating with Linda changed into marked by way of the use of means of personal triumphs and tragedies. Together, they celebrated the transport in their daughter, Shannon, who have to skip immediately to come to be a a achievement businesswoman, writer, and determine of her father's legacy.

Throughout their marriage, Linda remained a steadfast and supportive presence, even within the face of the tumultuous u.S.And downs of Hollywood. She stood with the useful useful resource of Bruce as he worked on his mythical film "Enter the Dragon" and persevered to be a supply of strength and concept.

The tragic demise of Bruce Lee in 1973 emerge as a devastating loss that left Linda and their own family in mourning. It modified right into a second of profound grief and an abrupt finishing to a love story that had spanned continents and defied the chances.

The "Game of Death"

Unfinished Projects: The Game of Death

Bruce Lee became a person of imaginative and prescient, a creator who continuously pushed the bounds of his paintings. His quest for excellence turned into unrelenting, and he sought to task not excellent the norms of Hollywood however also the conventions of martial arts cinema.

In 1972, Bruce released into a modern day undertaking that would turn out to be known as "The Game of Death." It changed into to be a groundbreaking movie, a martial arts masterpiece that would embody his philosophy, combat talents, and imaginative and prescient. The film have become to be a testomony to his belief in constant evolution, every as a martial artist and as a filmmaker.

"The Game of Death" turned into no everyday undertaking. Bruce anticipated it as a current-day paintings that would introduce new thoughts and thoughts in martial arts cinema. It was a film that would challenge the restrictions of the style, and he have become determined to make it a magnum opus that might resonate with audiences international.

The Death of James Lee

Tragically, Bruce Lee's pursuit of his vision for "The Game of Death" modified into marked with the beneficial resource of a profound private loss. In 1973, he obtained the devastating information of the unexpected and sudden lack of life of his preferred brother, James Lee. James had been not fine Bruce's brother but moreover his confidant, training partner, and closest pal.

The lack of James turn out to be a profound blow to Bruce, who turned into left grappling with grief and the weight of private tragedy. It became a 2d of giant sorrow, one that examined his emotional resilience and left him in deep mirrored picture.

Despite the significant grief, Bruce Lee's indomitable spirit would not permit him to abandon his imaginative and prescient for "The Game of Death." He have become decided to honor his brother's reminiscence and to look the undertaking via to its very last contact.

Bruce Lee's Incomplete Vision

The making of "The Game of Death" changed right into a complicated and difficult method. Bruce had not best crafted a very unique and complicated storyline but had additionally designed a series of motion sequences that could display off the evolution of his martial artwork philosophy.

The movie grow to be purported to be a reflected photo of his center beliefs, a martial arts philosophy that became fluid, adaptable, and pragmatic. Bruce meant to apply the movie as a platform to hold the intensity and knowledge of martial arts past just physical fight. It changed into to be a metaphor for life itself, a adventure that required regular model, self-discovery, and the pursuit of excellence.

However, the of entirety of "The Game of Death" turn out to be marred with the resource of the usage of setbacks, which encompass Bruce's untimely dying in 1973. The mission changed into left unfinished, a testomony to the large challenges and complexities that Bruce had faced in the direction of its manufacturing.

The Legacy of the Unfinished Film

"The Game of Death" may additionally all the time live an unfinished project, a photograph of Bruce Lee's unfulfilled capacity and vision. The film have grow to be a reflection of his ceaseless pursuit of excellence, his belief in pushing barriers, and his relentless quest to redefine martial arts cinema.

Despite its unfinished nation, "The Game of Death" could skip without delay to come to be a first rate part of Bruce Lee's legacy. It may function a testament to his unwavering strength of mind to his craft, his indomitable spirit, and his ability to inspire others to are searching out their paths of self-improvement.

The legacy of the incomplete movie prolonged a ways past Bruce Lee himself. It may inspire a cutting-edge-day generation of filmmakers, martial artists, and thinkers who sought to keep his art work and honor his vision. "The Game of Death" turn out to be a reminder that even inside the face of adversity and incomplete journeys, the pursuit of excellence and self-discovery have grow to be a noble company.

Chapter 13: Return to Hong Kong

The Homecoming

In 1971, Bruce Lee decided that might trade the trajectory of his existence and career. He decreases back to his birthplace, Hong Kong, after a hiatus in Hollywood. It emerge as a moment of profound importance, a homecoming that would see him reconnect along together with his roots and leave an indelible mark at the Asian movie corporation.

For Bruce Lee, returning to Hong Kong became not only a geographical shift; it have become a pass returned to his cultural records, a reconnection with the land of his ancestors, and an possibility to assignment the recognition quo of Asian cinema. It was a desire that might pave the way for one in each of his most iconic movies.

"Way of the Dragon" and the Colosseum Fight

Bruce Lee's pass decrease back to Hong Kong resulted internal the appearance of "Way of the Dragon," a film that would move at once to turn out to be a martial arts traditional. He wrote, directed, and starred inside the film, taking innovative manage in a way that few had earlier than him.

The movie's crowning achievement end up a memorable combat scene in the Colosseum in Rome, in which Bruce Lee faced off toward the mythical Chuck Norris. This iconic war grow to be not only a physical confrontation but a war of philosophies and martial arts styles. It showcased Bruce's commitment to authenticity, practicality, and directness in combat.

"Way of the Dragon" turned into a testament to Bruce Lee's imaginative and prescient, a mirrored image of his dedication to elevating the standards of martial arts cinema. It changed into a movie that resonated with audiences not simplest in Asia but spherical the sector, firmly putting in Bruce Lee as a global martial arts icon.

Bruce Lee's Cultural Impact in Asia

Bruce Lee's skip returned to Hong Kong had a profound cultural impact, not definitely in the film enterprise organisation but within the broader context of Asian society. He represented a new breed of Asian hero, one which challenged stereotypes and redefined the photograph of Asian men on display.

His have an effect on extended past cinema, inspiring a technology of greater younger Asians to include their history and aspire to greatness. Bruce Lee turned into no longer best a martial artist; he become a image of satisfaction, empowerment, and cultural authenticity. He embodied the spirit of a changing Asia, one that changed into eager to break unfastened from colonial legacies and description its identity on its terms.

Bruce Lee's effect in Asia modified into furthermore political. He became a picture of cultural resistance and a voice for the ones looking for to say themselves in a international that had often marginalized them. His popularity in Hong Kong and throughout Asia become not handiest a count number variety number of entertainment; it come to be a cultural and political statement.

Reconnecting with His Roots

Returning to Hong Kong allowed Bruce Lee to reconnect alongside together with his roots profoundly. He immersed himself in Chinese lifestyle, language, and philosophy. He explored the wealthy tapestry of Eastern belief, delving into the writings of Laozi, Confucius, and other Chinese philosophers.

His connection along together with his roots changed into not genuinely intellectual; it modified right right into a non secular journey. Bruce Lee sought to understand the essence of Eastern philosophy and martial arts, exploring the concept of "Wu Wei" (handy motion) and the interplay of opposites.

This reconnection along collectively along with his roots changed proper into a transformative revel in for Bruce Lee. It allowed him to in addition growth his martial artwork philosophy, Jeet Kune Do, thru integrating the data of Eastern belief collectively together together with his sensible combat strategies.

The Final Year

The Mysterious Death of Bruce Lee

In the summer time of 1973, the arena changed into greatly surprised through way of manner of the surprising and tragic death of Bruce Lee. He had been at the peak of his profession, together together together with his movies and philosophy developing a profound impact on global way of lifestyles. His cross again to Hong Kong heralded a brand new era in Asian cinema, and his have an effect on continued to increase.

Yet, on July 20, 1973, Bruce Lee's life emerge as lessen brief in situations that could all the time shroud his mystery of loss of life. He died in Hong Kong at the age of 32, leaving in the back of a legacy that modified into although inside the making.

The reliable cause of death have become listed as "dying through misadventure," attributed to a response to pain medicine. However, the suddenness and unexplained nature of his passing fueled hypothesis, controversy, and a huge quantity of conspiracy theories that persist to this current.

Conspiracy Theories and Speculation

The mysterious sports surrounding Bruce Lee's death gave upward thrust to a plethora of conspiracy theories and hypothesis. Rumors and hypotheses abounded, starting from allegations of foul play to the supernatural. Some advised that he had been the victim of an historic curse, whilst others believed that he have been centered thru enemies within the martial arts global.

One idea proposed that Bruce have been poisoned, at the identical time as a few different claimed that he had been the sufferer of a vengeful assault. The speculations had been as numerous as they have been an extended way-fetched, reflecting the surprise and disbelief that a person of Bruce Lee's stature may additionally want to meet such an untimely prevent.

The enigma of Bruce Lee's loss of life served as a testomony to his enduring impact. He turned into now not handiest a martial artist and actor; he become a photo of cultural delight and defiance. His demise left a void in the hearts of heaps and masses, and the search for answers have emerge as a quest for closure.

A Life Cut Short: The Tragic End

Bruce Lee's demise at the age of 32 have become a poignant reminder of the fleeting nature of life. He had completed repute, broken racial obstacles, and inspired generations, however his adventure were reduce quick absolutely as he turned into accomplishing new heights in his career.

The tragedy of his loss of life turned into compounded via the lack of his son, Brandon Lee, in a comparable unexpected twist of fate years later. It become a double blow to the Lee own family and a reminder of the fragility of life.

The abrupt and mysterious nature of Bruce Lee's loss of existence left a lasting effect on individuals who had regarded him and on his global fan base. It changed right right into a moment of collective grief, a revel in of loss that transcended cultural and geographical barriers.

The Aftermath and Shockwaves

In the aftermath of Bruce Lee's loss of lifestyles, the shockwaves rippled internationally. His legacy persisted to growth, and his impact remained undiminished. He had grow to be a legend, an immortal decide within the annals of records.

Bruce Lee's philosophy, martial arts, and movies persevered to encourage individuals from all walks of existence. His have an effect on prolonged to new generations of martial artists, actors, and thinkers who sought to have a look at in his footsteps.

His enduring legacy turn out to be marked by using the Bruce Lee Foundation, installation by using his daughter, Shannon Lee, to hold and sell her father's legacy. The basis's mission end up to honor Bruce Lee's paintings and philosophy and to hold ahead the values he had championed.

The shockwaves of Bruce Lee's loss of life may not fade with time. Instead, they may preserve to reverberate, inspiring people to venture convention, pursue excellence, and encompass their specific identities.

Chapter 13: Legacy In Martial Arts

Bruce Lee's Impact on Martial Arts

Bruce Lee changed into no longer merely a martial artist; he have emerge as a modern strain that reshaped the arena of fight sports sports sports activities. His impact on martial arts transcended the bodily realm and touched the very middle of the world. He changed right into a catalyst for trade, a discern who challenged conventions, and a visionary who redefined the possibilities of human fulfillment.

At the coronary coronary heart of Bruce Lee's impact on martial arts grow to be his martial philosophy, Jeet Kune Do. It became a philosophy that emphasised adaptability, directness, and practicality. He believed that martial arts need to no longer be limited by manner of manner of inflexible paperwork and traditions but should be a residing, evolving expression of individuality and effectiveness.

Bruce Lee's philosophy now not simplest inspired infinite martial artists however furthermore induced the start of a present day generation in combat sports sports. It shifted the focus from adhering to lifestyle to searching out what worked in workout. It encouraged martial artists to interrupt free from dogma and discover the big possibilities of combat.

The Evolution of Martial Arts in His Wake

Bruce Lee's philosophy ushered in a brand new technology of martial arts. His emphasis on adaptability and performance paved the manner for a greater complete approach to fight. Martial artists began out to pass-teach, incorporating techniques from numerous disciplines, and adopting a greater eclectic method.

This shift in martial arts philosophy gave rise to hybrid martial arts, in which practitioners discovered from in reality one of a kind patterns to create greater nicely-rounded and adaptable opponents. It caused the development of contemporary martial arts structures like Mixed Martial Arts (MMA), which emphasised versatility and practicality in the ring.

Modern Martial Arts: A Bruce Lee Legacy

The legacy of Bruce Lee in cutting-edge martial arts is profound. His philosophy laid the inspiration for a number of the martial arts practices and competitions we see in recent times. He championed the idea of non-save you self-improvement, self-expression, and innovation in martial arts.

One of the hallmarks of Bruce Lee's legacy is the emphasis on physical health. He understood that a robust and agile body emerge as important for martial arts skills. Today, his education techniques and exercising exercising exercises hold to encourage athletes and martial artists alike.

The philosophy of Jeet Kune Do additionally left an extended-lasting imprint on modern martial arts. It encouraged a thoughts-set of adaptability, the willingness to analyze from precise resources and the non-stop quest for self-improvement. This philosophy has had a profound have an effect on on martial arts instructors and practitioners global.

Bruce Lee's Influence on MMA

One of the most excellent affects of Bruce Lee's legacy is on the world of Mixed Martial Arts (MMA). MMA, with its severa style of combating patterns and strategies, embodies the adaptability and practicality that Bruce Lee endorsed.

MMA combatants nowadays often consist of things of Jeet Kune Do into their schooling, emphasizing directness, overall performance, and flexibility of their combating fashion. Bruce Lee's effect may be seen in the way MMA combatants method their craft, usually searching for to adapt and enhance.

Bruce Lee's philosophy and method to martial arts preserve to encourage the trendy generation of MMA warring parties. His emphasis on individuality and the merging of severa strategies is on the heart of current MMA, in which warring parties are not restrained to a single style however are recommended to be bendy and adaptable.

Cultural Icon and Philosopher

Beyond Martial Arts: Bruce Lee's Philosophy

While Bruce Lee is properly referred to as a martial arts icon, his legacy extends a protracted way past the world of physical combat. He became a truth seeker, a thinker, and a seeker of truth. His philosophy turn out to be a profound exploration of the human spirit, the character of lifestyles, and the pursuit of excellence.

At the coronary heart of Bruce Lee's philosophy became a determination to self-discovery and self-expression. He believed within the electricity of individuality and the importance of breaking loose from barriers. He noticed martial arts not simply as a way of self-protection but as a automobile for personal boom and self-actualization.

Bruce Lee's philosophy emphasised adaptability, the readiness to evolve, and the rejection of dogma. He entreated human beings to be like water, ever-converting and formless, capable of adapt to any scenario. His philosophy changed right into a name to motion, a name to live authentically, and a name to include lifestyles's disturbing situations as opportunities for growth.

The Influence of Taoism and Zen

Bruce Lee's philosophical underpinnings were deeply rooted in Eastern concept, especially Taoism and Zen Buddhism. He studied the works of Laozi and Chuang Tzu, finding in their teachings a profound information of the character of life.

Taoism's emphasis at the herbal go with the drift of lifestyles and the harmonious interplay of opposites resonated with Bruce Lee. He observed in Taoism a manner to stay in stability, embracing the dualities of life with out attachment.

Zen Buddhism, with its hobby on mindfulness and being gift within the second, moreover left a long-lasting impact on Bruce Lee. He believed that the vital thing to mastery lay within the capacity to definitely have interaction within the gift, to be inside the now, and to act without hesitation.

The Tao of Gung Fu

Bruce Lee's exploration of philosophy introduced approximately the advent of "The Tao of Gung Fu," a philosophical treatise that fused martial arts and Eastern idea. In this paintings, he tested the standards of martial arts in the context of philosophy, exploring their deeper which means that and implications for existence.

"The Tao of Gung Fu" modified into now not only a guide for combat but a manual to living. It explored the thoughts of centering, simplicity, and directness in martial arts and their application inside the broader context of existence.

Bruce Lee's philosophical writings, which incorporates "The Tao of Gung Fu," served as a testament to his intellectual intensity and his dedication to increasing the horizons of martial arts. He believed inside the electricity of concept and the potential of philosophy to form one's movements.

Bruce Lee as a Cultural Icon

Bruce Lee's cultural impact extended past martial arts and philosophy. He have end up a global cultural icon, a image of empowerment, and an advise for breaking racial stereotypes. His presence on show challenged conventional notions of heroism and masculinity.

Bruce Lee's air of mystery, strength, and air of mystery have been magnetic. He broke via the barriers of language and way of lifestyles, transcending borders and provoking people international. His legacy in movie have become now not restrained to martial arts; he have become a photo of a converting global, one wherein people must challenge conference, study their paths, and shatter the constraints imposed via the use of society.

His have an impact on have emerge as profound and a protracted way-task, touching the lives of people in severa fields, from sports activities activities to amusement to philosophy. He turned into now not most effective a martial arts hero; he changed right into a cultural icon whose legacy maintains to inspire generations to inside the meantime.

Bruce Lee's Enduring Popularity

Posthumous Releases and Documentaries

Bruce Lee's affect did not decrease collectively alongside along with his untimely dying. His legacy persisted to broaden and evolve within the years that observed. The posthumous releases of his films and documentaries chronicling his life introduced new generations to the enigmatic martial artist.

One of the most great posthumous releases modified into "Enter the Dragon," a movie that catapulted Bruce Lee to worldwide stardom. It have become launched just days after his lack of life, and it remains a timeless conventional, a testomony to his outstanding martial arts prowess and air of mystery.

Documentaries like "Bruce Lee: The Man and the Legend" and "The Life of Bruce Lee" delved into the depths of his lifestyles and philosophy, supplying insights into the individual within the again of the legend. These documentaries shed mild on his struggles, his relentless pursuit of excellence, and his enduring impact on martial arts and famous subculture.

The Bruce Lee Action Figure

The enduring recognition of Bruce Lee extended past the arena of cinema and documentary. He have become an movement determine, every literally and figuratively. His iconic reputation delivered about the advent of motion figures, taking pictures his likeness and martial arts prowess. These figures allowed fanatics to recreate their preferred Bruce Lee combat scenes and pay homage to their hero.

The motion figures symbolized the indomitable spirit of Bruce Lee, encouraging human beings to channel his electricity and determination. They served as a tangible example of his impact, inspiring new generations of martial artists and movement enthusiasts.

The Bruce Lee Brand

Bruce Lee's legacy extended to encompass a emblem that represented his philosophy and spirit. The Bruce Lee brand changed into now not most effective a business corporation enterprise; it embodied the values that he held luxurious, in conjunction with self-expression, adaptability, and the pursuit of excellence.

The Bruce Lee brand covered apparel, add-ons, and products that allowed people to encompass his philosophy and convey it with them in their each day lives. It have become a photograph of empowerment, a reminder that the spirit of Bruce Lee modified into alive in people who wore his call and photo.

The Eternal Appeal

The enduring recognition of Bruce Lee can be attributed to his ordinary enchantment. He transcended cultural, geographical, and generational obstacles, inspiring humans from all walks of existence. His philosophy come to be not confined to a particular time or location; it spoke to the timeless aspirations of the human spirit.

Bruce Lee's philosophy of adaptability and individuality remained relevant in a worldwide that constantly evolving. His message of breaking unfastened from limitations and embracing one's strong factor endured to encourage people in numerous fields, from martial arts to entertainment to private development.

His martial arts prowess, air of mystery, and the general subjects of his movies ensured that he remained a cultural icon, cherished through lovers spherical the arena. The enchantment of Bruce Lee have turn out to be eternal, a testomony to the enduring electricity of a person who had left an indelible mark on the sector.

Chapter 14: Pop Culture References And Homage

The Infiltration of Bruce Lee in Pop Culture

Bruce Lee's effect has become now not constrained to the realms of martial arts and philosophy; it permeated the very fabric of well-known way of life. His magnetic air of thriller, unheard of martial arts abilties, and profound philosophy infiltrated the worlds of film, television, track, and literature, leaving an indelible mark that keeps reverberating in modern-day media.

Films, TV Shows, and Music

Bruce Lee's presence in well-known tradition is most significantly felt inside the multitude of references, homages, and tributes that have emerged in movies, TV suggests, and music. Filmmakers and writers from spherical the arena has paid homage to the martial arts legend through way of incorporating his likeness and philosophy into their paintings.

The movie "Kill Bill" directed through the usage of Quentin Tarantino is a pinnacle instance of the have an impact on of Bruce Lee on cutting-edge-day cinema. Tarantino's artwork is imbued with a deep appreciation for martial arts and well-known way of life, and he regularly references Bruce Lee in his films. Uma Thurman's individual, The Bride, emulates Bruce Lee's iconic yellow jumpsuit from "Game of Death" in one of the film's unforgettable scenes.

Television indicates like "The Simpsons" have additionally celebrated Bruce Lee's legacy. The energetic series regularly will pay homage to iconic figures in famous way of life, and Bruce Lee is not any exception. In one episode, Bart Simpson wears a yellow jumpsuit similar to the only made well-known through using manner of Bruce Lee, further solidifying his recognition as a popular way of life icon.

Musicians, too, had been stimulated through Bruce Lee's air of thriller and philosophy. The rock band Queen paid tribute to him in their hit song "Dragon Attack," providing lyrics that alluded to his martial arts prowess and mythical reputation.

Bruce Lee's Enduring Presence in Modern Media

Bruce Lee's enduring presence in cutting-edge-day media is a testomony to his timeless enchantment. His films, philosophy, and iconic picture keep to resonate with new generations of enthusiasts. In an age of hastily converting trends, he stays a regular, a determine who transcends time and place.

The martial arts legend's philosophy of adaptability, self-expression, and the pursuit of excellence keeps to inspire individuals in numerous fields. His teachings have located their way into self-assist books, manage seminars, and motivational speeches, reinforcing his popularity as a cultural touchstone for private improvement.

His martial arts philosophy, Jeet Kune Do, has no longer high-quality motivated martial artists but has furthermore been embraced through law enforcement companies and navy gadgets looking for green fight techniques. His teachings, emphasizing practicality and directness, have resonated with those in professions in which precision and effectiveness are paramount.

The Bruce Lee Phenomenon

The enduring presence of Bruce Lee in modern-day media and famous way of life can most effective be defined as a phenomenon. His affect has lengthy gone beyond mere reputation; it has come to be a residing strain that continues to shape the area of amusement, philosophy, and private development.

Chapter 15: Bruce Lee's Unfinished Business

What Could Have Been

The untimely death of Bruce Lee on the age of 32 left the arena brooding about what might have been. He had completed international stardom, shattered racial obstacles, and transformed the martial arts landscape. But at some point of his meteoric upward push, his lifestyles have become lessen short, leaving many to invest about the unfulfilled functionality of someone who had defied conventions and challenged norms.

What could have been if Bruce Lee had lived longer? It's a question that lingers in the minds of people who favored his martial arts prowess and philosophical facts. He had already redefined the area of amusement and martial arts, and his starvation for innovation advocated that he end up on the brink of even extra accomplishments.

Unexplored Avenues: The Man and the Legend

Bruce Lee's life become a dichotomy of the person and the legend. On the handiest hand, he have become a deeply introspective reality seeker, a martial artist who sought self-development, and a committed family man. On the opportunity hand, he have turn out to be a cultural icon, a charismatic actor, and a photo of energy and empowerment.

The unexplored avenues of Bruce Lee's life are a testament to the duality of his lifestyles. He end up more than the jobs he completed in films or the martial arts he mastered. His unwavering dedication to personal increase, his quest for self-discovery, and his choice to empower human beings to stay authentically have been elements of his lifestyles that remained uncharted territories.

Bruce Lee's Perpetual Relevance

Bruce Lee's enduring relevance is a testomony to the undying nature of his philosophy and teachings. In an ever-converting international, his message of adaptability, directness, and individuality stays as pertinent these days as it changed into throughout his lifetime.

His philosophy maintains to encourage human beings from all walks of life, from martial artists on the lookout for self-development to leaders searching out revolutionary techniques. The resonance of his teachings transcends borders, languages, and cultures, illustrating the universality of his expertise.

The Ongoing Legacy

Bruce Lee's legacy is a residing, breathing strain that keeps to conform. It extends beyond the confines of a traditional biography, evolving inside the hearts and minds of those who have been touched through his existence and philosophy.

His ongoing legacy is clear inside the limitless martial artists who've been inspired thru his teachings, within the self-assist industry that keeps to encompass his thoughts, and within the well-known subculture references that pay homage to his effect. His enduring legacy is likewise obvious in the Bruce Lee Foundation, installation with the aid of way of his daughter Shannon Lee, which is dedicated to preserving and selling his philosophy and values.

Chapter 16: Reflecting On The Legend

The Impact and Controversy

The legend of Bruce Lee is a tapestry woven with threads of impact and controversy. His impact on martial arts, enjoyment, and philosophy is straightforward, but his lifestyles and legacy have also been the concern of intense scrutiny and debate. As with all iconic figures, the legacy of Bruce Lee is a complex one, marked through each profound effect and enduring controversy.

Bruce Lee's impact on martial arts is immeasurable. His philosophy of adaptability, directness, and self-expression transformed the way martial arts are practiced and taught. He challenged the conventions of conventional martial arts and endorsed a extra entire technique to combat.

In the arena of entertainment, Bruce Lee broke thru racial obstacles and stereotypes. He have become an international movie star, redefining the motion hero and shattering preconceived notions of masculinity. His films stay celebrated for their groundbreaking combat choreography and the air of mystery he brought to the show.

However, controversy has furthermore surrounded Bruce Lee's legacy. Some have stressed the authenticity of his martial arts talents, at the same time as others have raised worries about the accuracy of his lifestyles tale. The controversies have handiest brought to the enigma of Bruce Lee, sparking debates that keep to nowadays.

Bruce Lee's Place in History

As we mirror on the legend of Bruce Lee, it's far critical to bear in mind his place in information. He become a cultural icon who defied limitations, a truth seeker who challenged the repute quo, and a martial artist who left an indelible mark on his craft. Bruce Lee's location in facts is confident, now not clearly as an entertainer or martial artist, however as a image of empowerment and individuality.

His impact at the arena of martial arts endures, with martial artists of all disciplines embracing his philosophy of adaptability and directness. His have an effect on on the enjoyment enterprise stays palpable, with actors, directors, and choreographers normally stimulated by his present day approach to motion sequences.

Beyond martial arts and leisure, Bruce Lee's place in data is as a reality seeker who endorsed human beings to break free from barriers and pursue self-actualization. His teachings stay a supply of idea for the ones looking for non-public growth and self-improvement.

Assessing the Myths and Truths

The legend of Bruce Lee is observed thru a plethora of myths and truths, regularly interwoven in a tale that blurs the strains between truth and fiction. Assessing the myths and truths of his lifestyles is a complicated mission, as his legacy is shaped by manner of every reality and legend.

Bruce Lee have become certainly an awesome martial artist, renowned for his velocity, precision, and current strategies. His movies, which includes "Enter the Dragon," are celebrated for his or her impact at the vicinity of cinema and their contributions to martial arts choreography.

Yet, the myths surrounding Bruce Lee additionally persist. Stories of his unequalled fight abilties have sometimes taken on a mythic best, fueling debates approximately the authenticity of his talents. His existence story, marked thru stressful situations and struggles, has additionally been the hassle of hypothesis and fable-making.

www.ingramcontent.com/pod-product-compliance
Lightning Source LLC
Chambersburg PA
CBHW072157070526
44585CB00015B/1180